THE

Wall Street Retirement Conspiracy

A No-Nonsense Approach to
Retirement Planning

Philip Rousseaux

DISCLAIMER: Everest investment Advisors, Inc. ("EIA") and Everest Wealth Management, Inc. ("EWM") are affiliates. EIA is an investment advisor registered in the state of Maryland. EWM is an insurance agency licensed by the State of Maryland. Insurance (EWM) and investment advisor services (EIA) are two different financial products. EIA develops comprehensive financial plans for its clients, and that is the service we are offering. EIA believes that insurance may be (and usually is) an important part of such plans. Whereas EIA recommends to clients that they purchase insurance products (or enhance or supplement products they already own) the clients may purchase such products through EWM, although it is not mandatory they do so. Everest Wealth Management, Inc. is an independent insurance agency and, as such, only offers insurance products, including fixed index annuities. Everest Wealth Management is not an investment advisor and does not offer investment advice. Investment advisory services are offered by Everest Investment Advisors, Inc.

CONTENTS

PART I

WHAT
DOESN'T
WORK

PART I

CHAPTER 1

Wall Street Doesn't Work

You cannot hide from the reality of retirement. There is simply too much at stake when it comes to your well-being and security to ignore what is to come. Part I of this book will explore retirement planning tactics and strategies that do not work, and Part II will focus on tested solutions that have proven to be successful. I want to provide a clear picture of retirement preparation, and explain how to create a plan likely to carry you and your family safely and happily through your golden years. Unfortunately, there is a lot of bad information out there today, so I am here to dispel the myths and give it to you straight.

Today's financial industry is full of misleading information, and you deserve to work with a trustworthy expert who can guide you in the right direction. This book is going to upset the individuals who are making money through the manipulation of the American people. Many of these individuals can be found on Wall Street, and their success is fueled by the myths they produce in an attempt to intimidate the public. Chances are you may be working with one of these people right now, and the fact of the matter is that they do not want you to know what I know.

Hard-working Americans pour their hard-earned money into the Wall Street machine on a daily basis. Sometimes these people win, but more often than not they lose because they do not know that the system is purposefully rigged against them. Having worked in this field for nearly twenty years, I have seen this sad truth first-hand. I worked for one of the largest mutual fund firms and one of America's largest life insurance companies, before going independent and starting my own firm. The sales meetings and product pushes that I witnessed during my time with these firms alone would be enough to write an entire book about. For example, in the late 1990s and early 2000s, the insurance company that I worked for owned a mutual fund management firm. If you worked with one of the insurance company's agents during this time to set up a retirement plan like an IRA, chances are that you invested in a fund managed by this management firm. What most people don't know is that, while the insurance company's employees had access to thousands of mutual funds, the commission that they made by selling funds managed by the management firm was more than that of any other fund. Do you think that there is a conflict of interest in this situation? You bet you there is! And the financial industry is full of landmine conflicts just like this. Just remember, if you are working with a company that develops and brands their own products, you may be putting your entire savings at risk so that a sales agent can make a higher commission. Retirement planning is my forte, and I feel passionately driven to share my knowledge with the public and work to correct the existing misinformation.

Let's look at a hypothetical example involving a couple whom we will call George and Elaine Young. The Youngs, both fifty-six years old, live in Maryland and have $1 million in investible assets. They are a likable, average couple. The Youngs have worked hard all their lives and are now beginning to consider retirement; however, like most people, they have been putting it off for a while. Let's face it: planning for retirement is serious business. It is neither fun nor glamorous; health, mortality, and lifestyle changes all need to be considered before it is too late. Despite how intimidating these topics can be, decisions made early in life will affect your final years. Your retirement years are a significant chunk of the time that you will spend here on earth, and—if planned for correctly—they can bring much relaxation and joy.

Now, the Youngs are entering the retirement red zone, which means that for them retirement is likely less than ten years away. George and Elaine are baby boomers, so they don't have a lot of time to make more earnings or wait for the market to turn around. This is a period in their lives when they need to be meticulously conservative; they can't afford to wager with creative new ideas. Unfortunately, they will also need to make some important decisions immediately; tough choices made now will affect the quality of the rest of their lives. Retirement planning must include worst-case scenarios and what-if planning; the Youngs could live for anywhere between five and forty more years. One never knows the number of his or her days, which makes planning for retirement endlessly complex.

Some people believe that planning is planning, and that any company can provide the basic structure needed to plan for retirement. Others believe that working with a well-known company will give them a better retirement. These are some of the industry lies and dangerous assumptions that I work against. A recent study published in 2010 entitled "The EBRI Retirement Readiness Rating™: Retirement Income Preparation and Future Prospects" found that nearly 47 percent of baby boomers run the risk of running out of money during retirement. You do not want to end up eighty-five years old with a bad back, broke, and living with your children in their basement. How will you earn a new income? How will you care for your loved ones and dependents? How will you pay for rent? Safeguard your health? You need the right advisement to prepare for this situation. After all, if you mess up your retirement, there is no second chance.

The Youngs are an example of a regular couple. Folks like them with ten years or less until retirement need to act with urgency because they have less room on their timelines, but everyone—regardless of age or situation—should have some idea of what they want their later years to look like.

George and Elaine feel this urgency. They have to consider important money decisions and don't have a lot of information to draw on. George's parents—a generation apart—lived on a fixed pension and an income annuity, but they had no real significant assets.

This kind of out-of-date system is the only model that the Youngs are familiar with. When George's father was in his mid-eighties, his car gave out and he was unable to tap assets to buy a new car because they were under the control of the insurance company. When he passed away, there was no inheritance for George. His parents felt a sense of security, but they had no control. This is no way to retire. You have a right to the ownership of the assets that you have worked so hard for. His father's approach reminded George of a young child tied to an allowance. The Youngs don't want to relinquish their freedom to a big name. They are looking for help in the form of a backbone, not a straightjacket, and they don't want to work with an insurance company.

One day, George and Elaine see a billboard for a large financial institution on the side of the highway. They know that this is a serious company, and they know it's trusted. They have seen convincing and witty commercials on television. They have also seen friends grow smaller amounts of money in mutual funds under their management, and they have even invested in similar brokerage firms themselves with decent results. Many of their friends have turned to Wall Street for their retirement. It is the popular thing to do and it seems high-class and sophisticated to them, so George and Elaine decide that this may be the way to go.

Here is the problem: the Wall Street path does not work.

Let me say that again. Wall Street does not work.

No amount of sugar could coat the realities of this truth. I would rather lay the situation out there so that everyone who has access to this book will understand the truth. The information I provide in this book will allow for the "un-sweetening" of the reputation of American financial markets.

Going to Vanguard or a mutual fund for your retirement is the biggest mistake a person can make. Having worked in the trenches of our economy, I have had an intimate inside view of how large financial companies operate. I do not believe that they have your best interests in mind. They can't be objective. They are working for the investors and shareholders of their company to market their products at any cost. The last people they are worried about are George and Elaine Young in Baltimore, Maryland.

What I set out to accomplish with this book is to expose the machine of Wall Street, showing you why it won't work for you and why you must not, under any circumstances put your life in the hands of that faithless machine.

So yes, George and Elaine have seen friends of theirs make money in mutual funds throughout their lives, and they have even made some money in mutual funds themselves. You might have too. Mutual funds are generally great investments. But the companies that carried you *towards* retirement—that made you rich *during* your working life—are not the best companies to carry you through retirement. In short, what got you to retirement will not be what carries you through the rest of your life worry-free. If there is one thing you need to take away from this book, it is to stop relying on Wall Street for your retirement income.

Most financial advisors are focused on the accumulation of assets; in other words, they are worried about getting you from youth to retirement with the greatest amount of wealth possible. Unfortunately, the advisor who saw you through your accumulation phase likely will not have the specialized skills necessary to get you through the "decumulation" phase. There are many different rules and regulations surrounding retirement. It is a legally precarious situation, and one that you need a retirement specialist to help you navigate.

Furthermore, Wall Street is a giant gamble. Stocks are like slots. Even the most capable analysts and economists make predictions that turn out completely wrong—and these are costly mistakes. Did the Ivy League Wall Street gurus predict the dot-com bubble or the collapse of the financial markets in 2008? No. This is not because they are frauds or cheats—it is because the economy is a living, breathing beast that rears its ugly head in a number of surprising, frightening, and impossible-to-predict ways. The economy is both a bull and a bear, and unless you plan to retire in a zoo, it isn't the proper place for your life savings.

The problem is that most of the advisors on Wall Street are not specialists. They deal with accumulation and the fast-paced rides of the day-to-day. Retirement is a whole different field. These advisors may mean well, but things change too impulsively in their profession, and you run the risk of running out of money prematurely. This brings harsh vulnerability to investors; your retirement needs consistency and safety, not the risk of foreign markets or final closing bells. When you retire, returns are not what matters; retirement income—and insuring that you don't run out of it—should be at the forefront of your mind as you approach retirement.

I'm not saying Wall Street is a completely terrible institution. It is a great tool for certain people. If you have thirty more earning years ahead of you and plenty of time to recover when your stocks take a plunge, Wall Street may work for you. But for people like George and Elaine, heading into the retirement red zone with a set base to stretch out for the rest of their lives—which could potentially be thirty years or more—Wall Street is not the solution.

I know that a lot of people have not heard these warnings—general financial news doesn't speak on a human level. There's a lot of misleading information on the Internet, and even more in pop news media. There is bad information that people exchange all the time by word of mouth, especially between the generations, because the way Wall Street works has changed so much. We hear constantly about scandals, insiders, payoffs, and schemes. You need something with integrity. You need something firm to help build your peace of mind.

Sadly, there's even bad information being thrown around by people in professions like mine who are known as experts. Some of the bad information is innocent, but some is meant to lead you astray. Finance is, often times, basic sales. Many advisors work in transactions. Others, like myself, build in relationships. You need more than a brand and a formula. You, the client, have a life beyond the trade pitch. I'm here to show you what the real information is, and to help you move towards a decision about what to do with your money that will let you live out the rest of your life with meaningful ease. That's the least you deserve after working so hard all these years.

One of the positive benefits of the recent recession—there are silver linings to every cloud—is that the public finally realized that Wall Street is not a safe place for general assets. People are a lot more careful when investing in stocks, as well they should be. Declining economic circumstances have chipped away at some of the market's intimidation factor. Just think, in the last decade the market has seen two corrections of 50 percent, and the NASDAQ is still trading 40 percent below its 1999 peak as of the writing of this book.

Now, what you need to remember is that this logic is especially valid for retirement. When you invest money for retirement, you don't have the same kind of leeway that you did when you were younger and engaging actively in the workforce. There is no time to recoup errors and losses later in life. Baby boomers need to understand the concept of the "Human Life Value." In short, as you get older, your value declines because your value is based on your earning power. In layman's terms, at retirement your value is close to zero because you will not be working any longer. Wall Street might be able to get you to the place where you can retire, but it will not sustain you. Wall Street can be risky at forty, but it is even more perilous at sixty-five.

For a regular couple like George and Elaine—individuals who have worked hard all their lives and have investible assets worth somewhere between $500,000 and $2 million—I don't believe that Wall Street provides a solution. If you take anything away from reading this book, please learn that, in my opinion, you should not   be working with a large bank or brokerage firm when planning and then entering retirement. Take it from someone who's been on both sides of the fence.

Big banks and brokerage firms have a conflict of interest when it comes time to making decisions about your money. The public doesn't understand why this is such an enormous problem because most people haven't been behind the scenes at these institutions, and those who have stay behind the scenes and protect what they know.

People like me are a valuable resource because we have been behind the scenes and we have left for better fields. We have decided that working through a big bank or a brokerage firm is not the way to serve clients—although it may have been a great way to serve our own wallets. We have made a moral decision to forge our own pathway instead. This pathway is far more conducive to helping honest individuals like George and Elaine Young.

And in this book, I will walk that path with you.

CHAPTER 2

Mutual Funds Don't Always Work

THE SECOND THING that you need to know when planning for retirement is that mutual funds are not always the best solution. They may not be ideal for retirees who are looking for lifetime income, especially those with over $100,000 in investible assets. Not all mutual funds are bad, but you need to understand where mutual funds make sense and where they don't.

From a tax standpoint, the structure of a mutual fund is inherently flawed. To put this in simple terms, mutual funds are pass-through entities; they do not pay taxes on earnings, but rather pass the burden of the taxes on to the investor. This may sound harmless, but believe me it is not. My years of experience in this field have taught me otherwise, and you have the right to know the truth.

First, let me make it clear that I am not discussing these tax issues in respect to IRAs or 401(k)s; I am focusing solely on mutual funds in nonqualified accounts. Now, let's assume that in a given year, there are more people who want their money out of a fund than people who want their money in it. This would lead to a disproportionate amount of sellers and buyers, which means that net flow to the fund is negative. This type of flow became more and more common with the economic downturn, and if there are more net out-flows than in-flows, then mutual funds are in trouble. As a result, mutual funds have to find a way to cover their redemptions, and the easiest way to do this is by selling stocks. Unfortunately, once they liquidate stocks, the tax burden on those sales is passed on to the shareholders—whether or not those shareholders participated in the upside.

Imagine that I start a mutual fund. We'll call it the Phil Mutual Fund. Let's say I'm the only person who invests, and I decide to buy $1,000 worth of Google. Now let's assume that the stock of Google doubles, and the fund is now worth a total of $2,000. Then I get a new investor, Joe. He wants to buy into the mutual fund, so Joe puts in $2,000. At this point, we each own half of the mutual fund, which now has a total investment of $4,000. Later, I decide that it's time for me to sell Google. Once I do, Joe will get a 1099 from the Phil Mutual Fund for his share (50 percent) of the sale of Google ($1,000 capital gain). Joe then has to pay taxes on something he didn't even make any money on!

But that is only half of the story. Maybe I decide to buy Apple stock. Say I'm unlucky and buy the stock at $700 a share from Joe's cash and the proceeds of selling Google, but at the end of the year the stocks are each only worth $400. Both Joe and I have lost money. You may be shocked to learn that, come New Year's, Joe will receive a 1099 from the Phil Fund for capital gains to the tune of $1,000. Remember, Joe's initial investment was $2,000, and now that is worth only $1,300. He didn't participate in the upside of Google's stock, and yet he still has to pay taxes on the $1,000 gain. Basically, Joe inherited the taxes from the mutual fund's initial investments. Again, mutual funds are pass-through entities that stick you with taxes instead of paying them. As you can see, they are clearly not tax-efficient.

This is only one example of mutual fund complications. We learned hard lessons on this very issue during the financial collapse of 2008. As the market fell, mutual funds lost significant value—devastating thousands of honest investors—and a lot of people sold in fear.

When mutual fund redemptions exceed inflows, this creates the need for them to start selling positions to raise cash. The fund managers, of course, decided to sell stock as an immediate source of funding during the 2008 crisis. This created a situation where the mutual fund now had gains (from the sale of the stocks), and so it needed to tax the shareholders. Investors lost money—as much as half of their holdings in some mutual funds—but the mutual fund had gains from selling stocks, and sent 1099s to the investors. In the end, shareholders lost money and were then further taxed by the mutual fund's actions. They may not have participated in portions of the gains, but they paid for all of it, nonetheless, adding insult to injury.

Taxes are only one aspect of this argument. Another issue with mutual funds is known as *window dressing*. Most mutual funds do not disclose the entirety of their holdings, simply because they do not have to. The full list of entities is considered a trade secret, but they are required to show the top ten or twenty largest holdings, and update this list every quarter.

Many funds take advantage of the disclosure through the manipulative strategy of window dressing. At the end of a quarter—just before the mutual fund has to report its holdings—the fund manager will research the stocks they missed out on. If Apple's stock soared that quarter, but was overlooked in selection by the fund manager, he will buy as much as possible at the last minute so that the stock will show up in the mutual fund's top holdings. As a result, potential and current investors will assume the fund manager is on top of market trends, responsible, and that this is a fund worth owning. This will ease the investors into feeling that they have a qualified and trustworthy manager running their portfolio. In reality, however, the manager is only doing busy work; he is like a department store supervisor who has the best and brightest merchandise placed in a window display. All the world passes by impressed by the offering and eager to go inside for more.

Window dressing is unfair and leads investors astray by releasing a deceptive description of a mutual fund's performance. It is nearly impossible to gauge the actual quality of a fund when managers are so concerned with looking good.

Mutual funds also face heavy regulation and are bound by their prospectus and other laws. One of these regulations is that a fund can't own more than a certain percent holding in any single stock. This can cause the fund to be diversified to the point of inefficiency. It makes it difficult to maintain congruency within fund families, which, in turn, counters the likelihood of financial gains. One can liken it to "putting all the eggs in one basket." Most large company US mutual funds have between 300–500 positions, which is an unthinkably large amount to hold. While diversification is meant to add safety and is one of the selling points for a mutual fund, it can be counterproductive to the investing process as a whole. Why would a person want to own, for example, a portfolio with J. C. Penney, Macy's, Saks, Nordstrom's, and five other large department stores? That doesn't make sense—you want the very best of the breed. It is better to stay on top of your investments and nurture a few good ones rather than buy a tiny bit of nearly every single brand on the market. I'd choose to enjoy a few slices of the three best pies, instead of having a tiny bite from nearly a dozen. In short, I believe that investors should seek quality, not quantity.

So far, we have discussed taxes, window dressing, and over-diversification. These three factors alone give more than enough reason to avoid mutual funds, but the next factor is also the most important, and it truly drives the point home.

Nothing is more detrimental to your success as an investor than mutual fund fees. Some are disclosed, but a lot of fees are actually hidden. Most people don't know about these fees because they are well hidden. The banks and brokerage firms do an excellent job of burying information, making it difficult to find for shareholders. In the same way, there are embedded charges in all types of mutual funds. Funds add many different "extras" that you will pay for whether you like it or not. A lot of investors believe that if they are in no-load funds, they don't pay fees. This is a huge misconception. No-load funds may not have loads, but the firms that manage them are certainly not non-profit corporations.

The hidden fees work differently for 401(k)s and regular mutual funds, so I will begin with the regular mutual funds. These funds first have manager fees, which are used to pay the manager buying the stocks. According to the Investment Company Institute, the average mutual fund expense ratio in

[1] Bernasek, Anna. "What a Difference a Percentage Point Can Make." *The New York Times*. 6 October 2012. Web. 4 October 2013. <http://www.nytimes.com/2012/10/07/business/mutfund/mutual-fund-fees-are-declining-but-still-vary-widely.html?_r=0>

America is 1.44 percent[1]. This would be acceptable if it were the only fee one had to pay for management. Of course, it's not the only one.

The next fee is in the layered cost of a mutual fund: the fee for buying and selling stocks and bonds within the mutual fund. Because this fee does not have to be reported in any way by the brokerage firm or bank, almost no one knows about it, but I'm telling you now because I believe that the public has the right to be informed. This fee is known as the "trading cost." The average amount of this fee as of 2010, again according to Forbes, is 1.44 percent[2].

Together, manager's fee and trading costs add up to an average of 2.9 percent, a significant addition to the cost of owning a mutual fund. And remember, these are only averages; these fees can be higher or lower depending on the type of fund (international funds obviously have higher fees than US Government Bond Funds) and the fund family. Keep in mind that even no-load funds have these fees.

[2] Bernicke, Ty A. "The Real Cost of Owning a Mutual Fund." *Forbes.* 4 April 2011. Web. 4 October 2013. <http://www.forbes.com/2011/04/04/real-cost-mutual-fund-taxes-fees-retirement-bernicke.html>

There is another fee, that some firms charge, called a 12b-1, which is capped at 1 percent. This fee can be used to advertise a mutual fund, pay for a broker's commission, and offer compensation to wire houses who sell funds they don't manage.

Take a look at the following table as an example:

$100,000 INVESTMENT IN ABC MUTUAL FUND
Annual Cost

Fee Type	Fee Percentage	Total Amount Paid for Fee
Expense Ratio	1.41%	$1,410
Trading Costs	1.31%	$1,310
12b-1 Fee	1%	$1,000
Total:	3.72%	$3,720

If you held the sample fund above for ten years with no growth, you would end up paying a shocking $37,200! Even if you had an average growth of 9 percent a year—which is quite high—according to the table above, 41 percent of your returns would be eaten up by fees. That, to me, is complete insanity. And remember, you don't even see these fees on your statements.

Shockingly, there are more fees that we haven't even mentioned yet. For certain funds if you go below a certain dollar amount, you are levied an *account fee*. Some firms also charge a *redemption fee* if you buy and sell within a short time frame. In addition, consider the exchange fee, which is charged when you move money to other accounts, and the purchase fees. There are obviously more fees and expenses associated with owning many mutual funds than anyone might expect and it's often difficult to find an explanation of these fees.

401(k)s have even more exhaustive fee schedules, most of which mutual funds aren't required to report. These charges are rarely mentioned, and many financial experts even have trouble figuring them out. You could be hit by *legal fees, trustee fees, stewardship fees, bookkeeping fees,* and *finder's fees.* I know all of this sounds ridiculous, but this is a normal part of the mutual fund system. The extra charges, as I have explained, will eat into every penny of the savings you have managed to store away.

The mutual fund industry is a billion-dollar behemoth. Lately, there have been efforts from Capitol Hill to try to reduce the additional and excessive fees, but the attempts at fair legislation have been stymied by the powerful Wall Street lobbyist machine. Sometimes mutual funds don't even disclose their fees to the government.

The truth is, when you're paying fees between 2 and 4 percent, it's hard to make money in the long term—especially in such a volatile market. You also have to ask what you are getting for these fees. Is there ongoing financial planning advice? How about tax management planning? Do you sit down and talk face to face with your brokerage firm on a regular basis? Do they call you to update you on your account on a quarterly basis? Do they make changes based on your aging and needs? Probably not.

You might already be convinced that mutual funds are perilous, and these reasons alone would be plenty—but there's more. It continues with what I call the *myth of annual returns.* This is the falsehood that mutual funds always provide in an annual return of, for example, 10 percent. Things are not really how they appear to be. Wall Street is a great marketing machine, and they have figured out how to promote average returns in a very appealing way, but the truth is very, very different.

It's very important that people understand the difference between the *average* annual rate of return and the *actual* rate of return. For example—look at the Dow Jones Industrial Average between 1931 and 1950. In that era, the average annual rate of return was 5.26 percent. If someone were to do a quick calculation online to see how a $100,000 investment would do with those rates, the account would be at $290,357 by 1950. But here's the twist—that fictional account would have really only been worth $143,154. And this calculation, mind you, assumes no fees. That's almost a 50 percent difference. The actual rate of return was 1.81 percent, not 5.26 percent, due to volatility. Just as I described in the paragraph above, the average and the actual returns are very different. Dangerously different.

The last mutual fund issue to discuss is based on my personal philosophy and strategy. When you look at the history of large-cap mutual fund managers in the US, 80 percent[3] of them underperform the benchmark, the Standard & Poor's 500 Index. The reason for this is believed to be due to the large amount of information and data readily available about these publicly traded companies. If 80 percent of the active managers don't outperform the index, why would you invest in anything but the index? Now, remember, it's not possible to invest directly in the index; however you can invest in a mutual fund that seeks to track the index. You can also invest in "Exchange-Traded Funds" such as the iShares S&P 500 ETF. The best part about these ETFs is that they don't have many of the issues that affect mutual funds. The fee on the iShares S&P 500 ETF is seven basis points—that's .007 percent! Compare that fee with most of the large-cap mutual fund fees that

---

[3] Wharton School of Business. October 2013. CIMA® Class, Dr. Craig MacKinlay.

range between 2 and 3 percent. Do you know the difference that layered fee, with no return to justify it, can make? If you invested $100,000 and earned a 7 percent return for twenty years in the ETF, you would have an amazing $381,936 net of fees. Now, imagine you invested in a large-cap mutual fund and they matched the returns of the index, which we already know 80 percent don't do, but let's assume they did. The mutual fund that returned 7 percent would only be worth $219,111 net of those heavy fees. That is a $162,000 difference, and it's one that most Americans are exposed to by using actively managed large-cap mutual funds in their IRAs, 401(k)s, and brokerage accounts. Keep in mind that the ETF is also tax friendly. They trade as stocks on the exchanges so the investor has a lot more control of the taxes paid on his or her investment; you simply pay taxes when you sell the ETF. Do you still believe in active management? Wall Street wants you to. Imagine if all those people stopped owning those investments; the fees lost would be enormous!

It's not that we don't believe in owning equities and a stock portfolio, it's that we believe if you are going to go down that path, you should be aware of the fees you are paying and the management that you are paying for. There are certain markets where an active mutual-fund investment policy would potentially make sense such as with a small company or international investing in emerging markets. The data supports that active management in these areas can add value and justify the higher fees they charge as opposed to investing passively in index funds or ETFs.

If you are looking to invest in the market, you should also be aware of historical returns. I don't believe the returns we have seen in the last twenty years are realistic; going forward you should expect lower returns and here is why. First, over the past thirty years, we have experienced unprecedented returns on bond investments, both on the corporate end and in US government bonds. The reason for this is because inflation went from the mid-teens in the 1980s to below 3 percent in recent decades. As the Federal Reserve made changes and lowered interest rates, this helped start the longest bull run in bond investing that we have seen in the last one hundred years. You see, every time the Federal Reserve lowered interest rates, the bonds values that have higher coupon payments went up. The long-term return on government bonds has been two to three times what it should be, and this is the main reason why. The catalyst has been a thirty-year interest rate decline.

Real Returns on Bonds (Compound average real returns)		
Period	Medium-Term Treasuries	Long-Term Treasuries
1981-2012	5.0%	7.2%
1951-2012	2.4%	2.6%
1926-1950	1.9%	2.7%
1926-2012	2.3%	2.6%
Source for data: Ibbotson Associates. The medium-term bond is a 5-year Treasury and the long-term bond is a 20-year Treasury.		

As you can see from the chart above, from 1926–1981 long-term government bonds' real returns were around 2.6 percent, which is a big difference from the 7.2 percent from 1981 onward. I expect that interest rates will remain somewhere close to where they are, or perhaps move somewhat higher, but it will not be possible to have returns on bonds like we have seen for the last thirty years without interest rates going down, and they can't go much lower.

Secondly, let's dive into US equities, or large-cap stocks. Again, I believe, and the data will support, that real returns on US stocks typically run around 6 percent. Now, most investors out there are used to what they know and what we have seen, and from 1981 until 2000 the large-cap stock market had real returns of 11.6 percent! (See chart on the following page.) This is almost double what the return had been from 1926 to 2012! I believe that returns will be lower going forward. The past decade is often referred to as "The Lost Decade" because we did not experience returns and saw two 50-percent-plus drops in the major US indexes. I believe that a good explanation of this "Lost Decade" is that it

Real Returns on Stocks	
Period	Large-Cap Stocks
1981-2000	11.6%
1981-2012	7.2%
1951-2012	6.8%
1926-1950	6.3%
1926-2012	6.6%
Source for data: Ibbotson Associates and S&P	

is helping us to revert to the mean return, which is closer to 6 percent, not 11 percent.

Investing in stocks takes skill, and it's not something you can learn in a weekend or by taking a day-trading class or even reading a book, so most people invest in mutual funds. The most difficult thing isn't just what investments to buy, it's when to sell, and how to sell. You have to be disciplined, educated, and a professional. You also need to be wary of hiring others to do it for you, because more times than not, you are paying extra fees for lackluster performance and driving down your overall return. You also shouldn't be investing in stocks for essential income if you are a baby boomer; it's a huge mistake! I think by now I have given you enough caution about mutual funds. Next, we will discuss another misstep that many take while investing for retirement.

CHAPTER 3

Why Variable Annuities May Not Be the Right Tool

WE HAVE ALREADY discussed why Wall Street and mutual funds are not effective tools for retirement investing. In this chapter I will discuss a third popular option for retirement investing—variable annuities—and explain why this tool may also not be the best place to put your hard-earned savings.

Let's start with the basics. One of the biggest downsides to variable annuities is that most people—including those who sell them—don't fully understand how variable annuities work. To put it in the most basic terms, a variable annuity is a contract between an investor and an insurance company. John Hancock, MetLife, and Prudential are examples of some of the big companies out there that sell variable annuities. Variable annuities have been around for a long time, and they worked a lot better a few generations ago. They were originally a tool used to shelter high-tax-bracket individuals from long-term dividends and capital gains, but this was back in the 1970s and 1980s when the rates were as high as 30 to 50 percent. Now that tax rates are much lower, at around 15 percent, variable annuities aren't nearly as useful. They are also a negative choice for a number of other reasons, which I will detail in this chapter.

The good thing about variable annuities is that you can put an unlimited amount of after-tax dollars into them. In this way they are an improvement over IRAs, where you can only add a limit of, say, $5,000 a year. With variable annuities you could put in, for example, $3 million after taxes, which would shield returns on that money from capital gains and taxes. This basic idea is the main selling point for all annuities, variable annuities included. The dangerous difference with variable annuities is that the investor (not the insurance company) bears most, if not all, of the investment risk.

Within variable annuities there are "sub-accounts," which contain many of the same elements as mutual funds. For example, you can buy a fund by the name of the Fidelity Spartan Fund from both Fidelity and from an insurance company for an annuity. These are technically different funds, but you would have the same manager, the same premise, and they would buy the same securities. The difference is that in the annuity, the money grows tax-deferred until you can take out the funds, which is usually at the age of fifty-nine and a half.

Now, as you will see, variable annuities are exceedingly complicated. That is part of the problem with them, as I mentioned above. Customers are often duped by the confusing nature of the funds and have trouble understanding what is really being offered. I used to sell variable annuities, and through my years working with a major company, I found that many people who sell variable annuities don't even actually know what they are. This might sound shocking, but it's true. If the person selling you the annuity doesn't even understand it, it is very unlikely that you will be able to understand it; an average investor often has a lot of difficulty understanding all the moving parts of variable annuities.

Besides the confusing nature of their structure, another major downside to variable annuities is that the fees are tremendously high. It's not uncommon to see the internal fees on variable annuities running from 4 to 7 percent a year, and sometimes they can be even higher. People don't realize just how many fees they are dealing with because these fees are not stated as an up-front charge. As is the case with mutual funds, these fees are often buried in the prospectus, which is hundreds of pages long and exceedingly complicated to understand. Even if you know where to look for the data, you will have quite a lot of trouble finding what you need. Companies often fail to include values in their examples in order to make the information even more inscrutable.

For the purposes of exploring the fees in this chapter, we will look at the MetLife Preference

Plus Select Variable Annuity prospectus from May 1, 2009. These prospectuses don't change terribly often, and they are available publically online. Now, the first thing to note about this prospectus is that it is 822 pages long. The sheer length begs the question of who would sit down and read the entire document. And how would someone wade through all of this information, even if they were only seeking a specific data point? These documents are also incredibly complicated, and purposefully so. The companies don't use concrete examples to illustrate their points because they don't actually want you to find out the horrible truth: that your fortune is being slowly eaten away by fees.

We will look at the Bonus Class Annuity and assume an investment of $100,000, just as we have in previous chapters. First we will look at the basic fees and then move to the add-ons.

The first fee is the basic fee to open your account. MetLife charges an annual contract fee of $30, and people think that's all they pay. Sadly, that's basically the fee for them to mail you your statement.

Sometimes they'll waive that fee if you have more than $100,000 in your account, so our example investor may not have to pay that specific fee, but in comparison that fee is so insignificant that it hardly matters. Even though it's all that most people think they're paying, in reality it represents nothing; it's not even the tip of the iceberg, but just a snowflake.

The next fee is called the Basic Death Benefit Class or the Mortality and Expense Ratio (M&E). The average amount for this fee in MetLife's Bonus Class Annuity is 1.95 percent. This is a fee you will have to pay for just opening your account. For this fee, the company has agreed to guarantee a death benefit to your heirs of the original investment ($100,000) or the current account balance if it is higher. If the mutual funds lose value your heirs will get $100,000. If the mutual funds make money, your heirs would get that amount.

These kinds of variable annuity contracts can make sense in certain scenarios. Let's say that we're talking about someone who is eighty years old. They have $100,000 sitting in a CD. That person is losing money every year on their funds, and a variable annuity would make sure that they didn't lose any of their money. They are basically guaranteeing with the variable annuity that the beneficiaries will have at least what they have now. If they don't want to lose the money and they want their daughter to inherit it when they die, this could be a great plan. It would let them be aggressive and roll the dice, hoping to turn that $100,000 into $130,000 or $150,000. They could be sure that their daughter will at least get what they put in, and she might even get more. So as you can see, variable annuities can be a powerful tool as a death benefit for someone who is risk-averse.

Ever since 2008, however, a lot of insurance companies are underwater and on the hook for all of these death claims. Now many have changed their policies and they won't give you a variable annuity after the age of seventy-five or so because they don't want you to use it as a death benefit. And another thing to remember is that, even in the best of situations, you're paying a lot of money for that death benefit. The cost per year is $1,950 for our sample $100,000 investment.

The fee we spoke of—1.95 percent—is only an account fee. That fee basically just allows you to open up your account and nothing else. You have to then worry about the sub-accounts, which are the mutual funds and come equipped with their own long list of fees, many of them similar to what we discussed in Chapter 2. The mutual funds have manager fees of between 0.54 percent (for cash, bonds, and money markets), all the way up to 1.6 percent. If we take the median of those numbers, we're adding in another 1.1 percent to the fees that already exist. Mutual funds also have trading costs, which, as you may remember, are not disclosed in the prospectus. The average trading fee is 1.44 percent.

So let's do some simple math. You have the M&E fee, the first one that we mentioned, which is 1.95 percent. Then you have the sub-account management fee, which is 1.1 percent on average, and the 1.44-percent average trading fee. Already, you are at 4.49 percent, so you can see why I am not a fan of these fees.

And the fees don't even stop there. There are also optional riders that you can add to your package. Let's say we want an optional death benefit step-up that would provide the greater of either what is in our account on that day or any previous anniversary statement. If we take that rider, our initial fee will move from 1.95 to 2.15 percent. So now your total fees would be up to 4.69 percent. And take it from me, the salespeople at these insurance companies usually try to push the step-up death benefits. On top of all that, variable annuities have living benefit riders, which can range from 0.5 percent at the cheapest all the way up to 1.5 percent in this MetLife prospectus. If you add the most expensive living benefit and death benefit riders, well then you are up to 6.19 percent. That means you're down −6.19 every year automatically, which is a huge cut to your investment. You would be lucky to do a gain of 7 percent in the market every year nowadays, so that means with the best of luck, you're only gaining about 1 percent with the fund. The fee structure is so bad with these investments that it completely handicaps your ability to make any money in the market.

$100,000 INVESTMENT IN METLIFE VARIABLE ANNUITY — Annual Cost

Fee Type	Fee Percentage	Total Amount Paid for Fee
M&E Fee with Step-up	2.15%	$2,150
Average Management Fee	1.1%	$1,100
Average Trading Fee	1.44%	$1,440
Living Benefit Fee	1.5%	$1,500
Total:	6.19%	$6,190

Do all of these fees mean that variable annuities are bad investments? No. They are good in specific situations, like the examples I detailed earlier, such as with older people who want to leave money to someone after they die. That said, I do not believe they are the correct choice for baby boomers looking for retirement income. I should know. I used to sell them, and I know how the industry works, inside and out.

Here is some of the history of variable annuities, to provide some context. In the 1990s, living benefit riders came out for variable annuities. There are three classes of living benefit riders, and you have to understand all three of them. The first kind is called the Guaranteed Living Income Benefit (GLIB) or Guaranteed Minimum Income Benefit (GMIB.) Some people still have their money in these types of variable annuities, so some are still floating around, but they aren't typically sold anymore. Both names mean the same thing, and most of the people who sell these types of variable annuities don't even understand how they work properly. They are very complicated, but I will explain them to you in clear, easy-to-understand language.

The myth about these kinds of variable annuities is that a lot of people think that you get a 6-, 7-, or 8-percent minimum guaranteed return, and even more if the mutual fund does well. The truth is so far from that mythology that it's not even funny. The insurance company basically gives you a step-up every year for, say, 7 percent, or more if the mutual fund does better. Let's take a look at what would happen if you had $100,000 in a MetLife variable annuity and chose the GMIB step-up.

As we can see in the MetLife Preference Plus 2013 prospectus from April 29, 2013, the fees associated with the step-up death benefit are 2.4 percent before you even take the mutual fund fees into account. The mutual fund fees are a minimum of 0.53 percent and go as high as 9.71 percent. On top of these fees are the trading costs—which are not even reported—so the collective fees are quite hefty, to say the least.

With the GMIB, you get a guaranteed step-up of 5 percent compounded. You decide that this sounds great, and you put your $100,000 into the variable annuity. If the variable annuity does wonderfully and you don't need to take the step-up benefit, then you will be fine. You just take out the lump sum, and you're done. That's all hunky-dory.

The problem is if you actually have to use the minimum guaranteed step-up benefit. People think the money you get using this benefit is real money, but the truth is a different story.

Let's say your variable annuity didn't grow, and that now it's only worth $50,000. MetLife has promised to guarantee you the 5-percent step-up. Say that you do not touch the $100,000 for a minimum of ten years as required by the plan. That means that after ten years you would have $162,889. Most people think that because they have waited the required amount of time, and are now out of surrender, that they can take the money out.

Wrong.

You can't take the money out because your investment is no longer real money. The insurance company makes you annuitize the contract.

This kind of system was very popular for people in our grandparents' generation, but the system doesn't work well today.

So at the end of ten years you are left with $162,889. This comes out to $591 a month that the insurance company has to pay you, but the company only guarantees a payoff for five years at that sum. If you die before five years, your beneficiary will continue to receive the sum until five years have passed, and that's it. So let's say you were sixty when you put in the $100,000, and now you have $162,889. The only portion they've really guaranteed of the original $100,000 investment is $40,000. To put it simply, if you take the monthly payment of $591 and multiply that by twelve, and then multiply that by five years, you get $35,460. This is all the insurance company has guaranteed to pay off. Technically, as long as the investor is alive, the insurance company has to give him $591. He could live to a hundred or he could die at seventy-five. The only thing we know for sure is that he'll receive $35,460. He would have been better off taking the money out of the variable annuity, even though the mutual funds did so badly.

Basically, this kind of variable annuity is the wrong investment for most people. Once annuitized, it would take twenty-two years and eleven months, in our example, to get all your money back. That means that if you put the funds in at sixty, you would have to live to be nearly ninety-three to get all your money back! And that's not even counting the fact that the payments don't go up. If you take inflation into consideration, you're in trouble.

You have destroyed any chance you have at being financially successful with this investment. What's more, you're giving up your asset. This means that you do not have the ability to take out extra money if you end up with additional expenses. In addition, your beneficiaries have no access to the funds after those first five years, which is such a small portion of the grand total. If you die within five years, the only person making money on the whole deal is the person that sold it to you. This is highly unfair, considering you're the one who earned all those savings to begin with. All of this information is what the fine print won't tell you.

So that explains the GLIB, which was the first wave of riders that came out. The next generation of riders was a little different. These were called Guaranteed Accumulation Riders (GARs), and luckily they are a lot easier to explain. These riders guaranteed the money would be there, free and clear, with the ability to use it however you want. You put the money in, and you either get that money back or you get whatever you make in the mutual funds. Sounds pretty good, right. The problem is that there are not many companies that offer these kinds of annuities any more. There were two problems with this rider. The first is that the insurance companies put limitations on what you could invest in. You couldn't just put all your funds into the stock market; you had to use their pools, which would be very conservative. They would be packed with something like 40 percent bonds, so the risk to the insurance company was very low. The second problem was on the side of the companies. These contracts put a lot of companies out of business after 2008. Hartford was one of the biggest companies out there, but because of contracts like this, they went out of business. The companies didn't price these plans properly, and after the downturn they were on the hook for a lot more than they had planned for. Ever since the economic downturn, you can't find riders like these anymore.

The third phase of riders is the Guaranteed Minimum Withdrawal Benefit Rider (GMWB). With these riders, the insurance company will guarantee that the account will step-up, for example, by 5 or 6 percent no matter what happens, and they have removed the annuitization requirement. Let's say you put in $100,000 when you're fifty. You wait ten years, and your account has grown to $158,000. These riders guarantee that you can take out a set amount each year without annuitizing. With these plans, the amount you can take out depends on your age. For example, an individual between sixty and sixty-nine years of age might be able to take out 5 percent. For someone between seventy and seventy-nine years of age, it might be 5.5 or 6 percent, and for someone between seventy-nine and eighty-nine, it might be closer to 7 percent.

Let's say that at sixty, you start taking out income. You take out 5 percent, which adds up to $7,900 a year. Even if your mutual funds are only worth $90,000, the company will let you take out a percentage based on the original $100,000. You will see your account going down, but you won't lose control of the asset. Whatever's left in your account when you die will go to your beneficiaries.

The nice thing about this is that the payments continue the rest of your life, and you still have control of the asset. The downside is that you can never take out more than the percentage you're allowed. None of the variable annuities out there will let you have increases in your income until your account balance grows, and that's a big problem. I tell all my clients that you will not be able to live forever on what you could ten years ago. How will you live on that measly 5 percent during a twenty-or thirty-year retirement with increasing insurance rates and inflation? None of the GMWBs give you increasing income unless your account balance goes up by more than what you've taken out. For the companies, offering increasing income is simply too hard to do because of high volatility and fees. Just remember that one of the fees in that mutual fund is at 9.71 percent! When you have total fees between 4 and 7 percent, it is difficult to take out 5 percent and still have the funds grow. It is not feasible long-term. If you're using a rider like this, you will likely deplete your whole account until you have nothing left for your beneficiaries. In addition, you won't have access to more than 5 percent at once, which makes your buying power dangerously low because of inflation.

Basically, fees are by far the biggest handicap for variable annuities. Variable annuities are simply not a good investment vehicle for most baby boomers. End of story.

Luckily, as we will discover in Part II, not all annuities are variable annuities.

CHAPTER 4

The Guy Who Helped You Get Rich Can't Help You Stay Rich, So He Doesn't Work (Anymore)

For the majority of working Americans, there are two important periods of investing. The first is the accumulation period, which stretches for the entirety of your working life. This is the period during which you are saving and accumulating assets by putting money into 401(k)s and IRAs. This period doesn't automatically stop when you get older. Even at fifty years old and beyond, Americans continue to save. In fact, this is an even *more* accelerated period of saving, because the government gives you an incentive to put even more money away.

The second phase of investing can be called a lot of different things, but I like to call it the "decumulation phase." This phase is very different from the accumulation phase. Most people think they can use the same financial advisor for the decumulation phase that they used in the accumulation phase.

They could be a mistake.

The investment tools you used to accumulate your assets and to get you to retirement may not work during retirement itself. I will take this statement one step further to say that the professionals you used to get you to the point of retirement may not be the ones that you should use during retirement. The key to a successful retirement—one where you don't run out of money—lies in working with a specialist.

Think of it this way: You might have a primary care physician who can do a lot of things for you. You trust that doctor. He can prescribe antibiotics, test you for strep throat, and keep an eye on your weight, cholesterol, and blood pressure. He has a lot of useful tools to help you stay healthy during day-to-day life. But if things get more complicated, you have to look elsewhere. If you begin to develop lower back problems, for example, you are not going to have your primary care physician open up your back and perform disc surgery for you. That's not his job—it's not his specialty—so why would you trust him with such a complicated and delicate operation?

The same goes for retirement planning. Why would you choose to work with a professional who specializes in accumulation and does not have a strong background in retirement planning? Even advisors who do work on retirement portfolios often work with three-dozen other types of investing scenarios as well. The most productive and safe route is to choose a specialist who focuses completely on retirement planning. Retirement planning is a very specialized field, and the tools and strategies used to create an effective retirement portfolio are very different than the tools used to prepare an effective portfolio during the accumulation phase. It is very difficult to be an expert in both of these fields; advisors who can do both are rare because the challenges of the jobs are very different.

The main difference between retirement planning and other types of financial planning is that retirement planning is not about making you rich, but rather about making sure that you don't go broke. This difference is key. The job of a retirement specialist is to focus on making sure you maintain enough assets and manage to get you a big enough allowance to keep you going through your thirty-plus years of retirement. This job requires very specific skills, which a regular financial professional is not going to have.

The first step I would recommend is to look for someone with a designation that focuses on retirement income planning. While working with a Certified Financial Planner® (CFP®) may seem to make sense—and it may be a good choice in some situations—it is not always the best approach. CFP®s are generalists that work in all areas, and, like we discussed earlier, you need a specialist rather than a generalist to help you through retirement. CFP®s often have specialties in other fields rather than focusing on retirement planning. Furthermore, a generalist is not going to be as skilled in any one specific field—that's just the nature of being a generalist. To be frank, you do not want to gamble on a CFP®'s competency when you are looking at preparing for one of the most important transitions you will ever make in your life.

A Retirement Income Certified Professional® (RICP®) is a unique designation geared towards retirement planning. I have found it to be much more appropriate than a CFP® for retirement planning because it is less broad-based and more specialized. Someone can be a CFP® and not be knowledge-able about retirement planning, but you can't be an RICP® and not be knowledgeable about retirement planning. The designation is specific to retirement planning skills.

As I said earlier, the challenges that you face when planning for retirement are very different than the challenges you faced during your working life. The biggest challenge is that your human life value—meaning your earnings—is gone. Your earning potential goes down to zero, and it becomes paramount that your specialist fully understands that your earning power is gone, and that you no longer have that human life power. Your professional needs to have the skills necessary to get you steady, solid income in all types of economic cycles. Whether you face expanding or contracting cycles during your retirement, you will need that steady income in order to survive.

One of the flaws I see all too often in my field is the huge amount of bad information in the media surrounding the systemic withdrawal approach.

There is extremely flawed information being disseminated on a daily basis about the systemic withdrawal approach. The way the approach works is that you go out and pick a withdrawal rate. You keep withdrawing at that rate and spending the same amount of money no matter what happens. You are usually forced to keep your money in extremely conservative funds in this approach. For example, a portfolio might contain 60 percent stocks and 40 percent bonds. From this, you then withdraw a flat rate each year. The average withdrawal rate used to be around 5 percent. Now that interest rates are lower than ever since the 2008 crash, some people are saying that 4 percent is a safer amount to withdraw; however, for this chapter we will use the

5-percent rate as an example, because that rate has been used over a larger expanse of time.

Banks claim that they've done Monte Carlo simulations to test these types of plans. This means that they back-tested the odds of someone running out of money using the example of a thirty-year retirement with 60 percent stocks and 40 percent bonds. Often these Monte Carlo simulations come up with fairly optimistic data. They show that the chance of running out of money in this scenario is between 0 and 5 percent, which sounds pretty good. These odds make it look like no one using this system will ever run out of money.

Sadly, that is not the case. The problem—which is a huge drawback—is that these companies are using historical data, which does not translate to today's economic environment. It is like I always say: if you put garbage in, you will get garbage out. If you look at fixed investments and where the rates are now, they are at sixty-year lows. If you go back thirty years to run a Monte Carlo simulation, you will find that interest rates were a lot higher and there wasn't nearly as much volatility. That's going to make the data look great, but the fact is that it's simply inaccurate for the current market. The probability of failure is a lot higher than they say because the companies are not taking into consideration two major pieces of information: interest rates are extremely low at the moment, and the market has more volatility now than there has been in over 100 years. Backtesting with this kind of data is akin to speeding down I-95 looking out your rearview mirror.

Another big problem these companies do not take into account is the timing of your returns. I call this factor the sequence of returns. This is the issue of whether you happen to retire at a bad time or a good time. Research now says that if you retire on a bad year, you will run out of money significantly faster than if you retire on a good year.

Let's take a look at the graph on the following page. This shows the difference between two people retiring on different years who both started out with $100,000 of retirement money using the same four returns. One of these people retired on the highest year in the sequence, and the other one on the lowest. Keep in mind that there is no way to predict when you will retire in a market cycle.

The person represented by the dark blue line on the graph retired when the market was at its lowest point in the sequence (-15). The person represented by the light blue line retired when the market was at its highest point in the sequence (+27). Despite the fact that they saw the same exact returns, the person represented by the dark blue line ran out of money thirteen years earlier than the light blue.

Thirteen years is a long time, and it is a lot of money to lose. And that was based on chance alone! One of these retirees ends up nearly broke about halfway through his thirty-year retirement, and the other retiree is completely fine.

The problem is that the average advisor out there won't understand the problem of the sequence of returns, and the truth is that it's one of the biggest issues out there when it comes to retirement investing. You can clearly see why you would not want to take the risk of keeping your money in an

Understanding the Sequence of Returns
The same market returns – but two different sequences

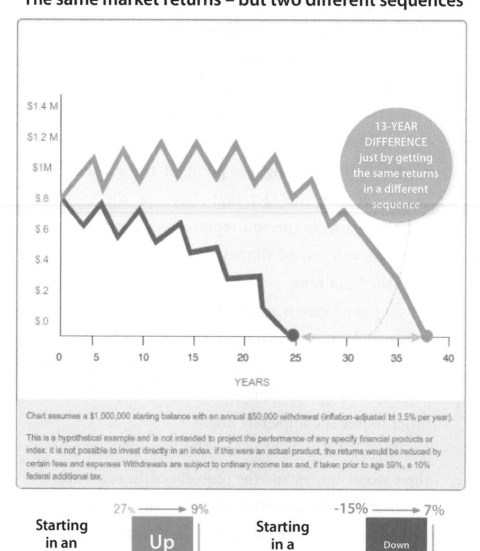

Chart assumes a $1,000,000 starting balance with an annual $50,000 withdrawal (inflation-adjusted bt 3.5% per year).

This is a hypothetical example and is not intended to project the performance of any specify financial products or index. it is not possible to invest directly in an index. if this were an actual product, the returns would be reduced by certain fees and expenses Withdrawals are subject to ordinary income tax and, if taken prior to age 59½, a 10% federal additional tax.

| Starting in an Up Market | 27% → 9% Up MARKET 15% ← 7% | Starting in a Down Market | -15% → 7% Down MARKET 27% ← 9% |

investment where there is such a high possibility of running out of money.

The fact is that the systematic withdrawal approach rarely works in the current economic environment. The people who say that it does work are flawed because you absolutely cannot take the Monte Carlo backtesting seriously. Factors such as lower interest rates and higher volatility make this testing extremely unreliable. The data gives you a false sense of security, which is extremely dangerous to the American public.

The other factor to keep in mind is that the average advisor out there is not going to look at factors like the sequence of returns, even though that is one of the biggest risks out there. The sequence of returns is not just a problem in your first four years of retirement. This issue can be a lifelong problem, and can have huge effects on retirees if they happen to retire on the wrong year.

Keep in mind that the graph above represents *the same four returns*. One client is broke twenty-five years into retirement—and twenty-five years is not a long time. For this to be a viable option, you would have to retire at sixty and die at eight-five. People rarely die at eighty-five anymore, which is why it is paramount to find a professional who understands problems like the sequence of returns. The sequence of returns is a real problem because you simply don't know what the market will do when you go to retire.

No one can confidently predict what the market is going to do. The fact is that you have to put in place safeguards against these risks. To accomplish this, you have to work with a professional who can effectively address these challenges. People predict when to retire based on their needs; they do not think about what the market is going to be doing. The best course of action is to work with a professional who can find solutions to protect you against the sequence of returns. You should be working with a retirement specialist, not someone who focuses on accumulation planning. Again, retirement investing poses a completely different set of challenges.

What are the chances your retirement income will last thirty years? If you're investing in stocks and bonds, the answer to that question will depend entirely on how the market performs. Let's look at the following graph to illustrate your chances of successfully making it through retirement without running out of money.

The following chart shows how long a hypothetical moderate-risk portfolio would last based upon when the retiree happened to begin his or her retirement. The blue bars show situations in which income would last thirty years or more, and the orange bars show situations in which the income fell short and the retiree would run out of money.

The retirees represented on this graph are using a systematic withdrawal approach and withdrawing 5 percent per year. The portfolios represented are made up of half stocks and half bonds, and are rebalanced annually. This graph takes into account historical data going from 1926 all the way up to 2009. The reason the graph only displays data from those who retired through 1979 is because this is the most recent retirement start date available wherein you can view a complete thirty-year retirement. Therefore, the data actually goes up until 2009—looking at people who have been retired at that point for several decades.

$500,000 Invested in a Moderate Portfolio, Withdrawing 5% Each Year

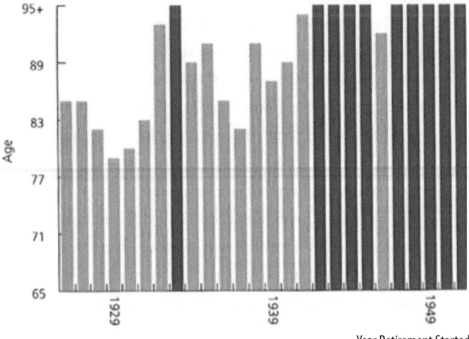

This is for illustrative purposes only and not indicative of any investment.

This image shows how long a portfolio would last based on 5% withdrawal rate on a $500,000 investment. It is assumed that a person retires at the year listed on the chart and withdraws 5% ($25,000) of the initial portfolio value, with withdrawals increasing by 3.10% annually to adjust to inflation. The inputs used are historical 1926-2008 figures; historical inflation of 3.10%; portfolio fees assumed to be 2%; moderate portfolio allocation (50% Large-Cap Stocks; 45% Intermediate Government Bonds; 5% T-bills). It is assumed that the portfolio is rebalanced annually.

Yellow - Ran out of money
Blue - Did not run out of money

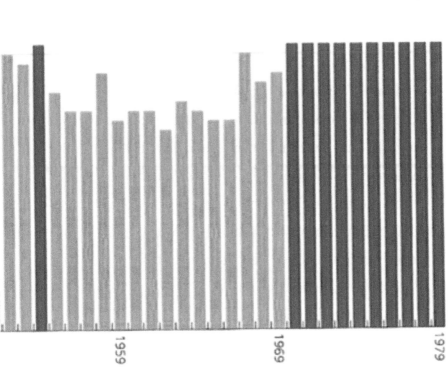

1959 1969 1979

Past performance is no guarantee of future results. Government bonds and Treasury bills are guaranteed by the full faith and credit of the United States government as to the timely payment of principal and interest, while returns and principal invested in stocks are not guaranteed.

About the data: Stocks in this example are represented by the Standard & Poor's 500®, which is an unmanaged group of securities and considered to be representative of the stock market in general. Government bonds are represented by the five-year U.S. government bond, Treasury bills by the 30-day U.S. Treasury bill, and inflation by the Consumer Price index. An investment cannot be made directly in an index. The data assumes reinvestment of income and does not account for taxes or transaction costs.

As you can see in this illustration, based upon all of the assumptions noted, retirees would run out of money nearly 60 percent of the time. I like to use this metaphor with my clients: Imagine you get on a plane. The pilot says, "Welcome to Generic Airlines. Everyone buckle your seatbelts. We will be landing in Cleveland in two and a half hours. The weather looks good, there's a slight updraft. The temperature in Cleveland is sixty degrees and sunny. Oh and by the way, statistically speaking we have a forty-percent chance of landing safely in Cleveland. There's a sixty-percent chance this plane will crash."

What would you do if you heard that announcement on the loudspeaker? Most people would get right off that plane without wasting any time. Let's apply that same thinking to your investments. Would you decide to invest with an accumulation advisor if he were using a strategy where 60 percent of the time you would run out of money?

PART II

SO WHAT DOES DOES WORK?

CHAPTER 5

Working With an Independent Firm Works

IN PART I, we looked at different systems of retirement investing that may not work for you. We touched on some of the most popular vehicles that Wall Street markets to Main Street including mutual funds and variable annuities. Additionally, we discussed financial advisors who are accumulation rather than retirement specialists.

By now, you are likely experiencing a distinct change in your outlook regarding prevalent investment beliefs. The marketplace is crowded with investment models and mutual fund ad campaigns, and you have likely accepted them as true in the past. After reading Part I, your notions of safety may no longer hold true, and this may be startling. Fortunately, there is a better way to invest for your future, but you aren't going to learn it from standard financial consultants. Luckily, teaching you these alternatives is the purpose of our work and the goal of the book that you are reading. In order to build lasting wealth, you will need expert guidance.

After leaving the big banks and insurance companies, I was determined to open a boutique firm; I wanted more in life than a business card. A smaller, personalized business would allow me to use my knowledge to make a difference in the day-to-day lives of real people. Providing a more intimate style of retirement income planning, I would be able to tailor and specialize retirement plans; I wanted nothing to do with the big-name style of grouping clients into a giant formula and thinking of them as nothing more than numbers. I committed myself to building a place where regular people could receive exceptional service that they would not find anywhere else.

I wanted to provide options that would truly allow for a successful retirement. This meant concentrating on maximized client gains while protecting the downside.

After much planning and preparation, I put everything that I had learned—and everything that I aspired to—into my own company. So how did I set my own company apart from other companies you may be accustomed to, and why should you look for a similar company for your retirement planning? Many great financial brands promote themselves as "different from the rest." While this is a wonderful statement, few advisory firms follow through. Being "different from the rest" requires dynamic action, individual care, and durable results. You want a company that looks at the stories behind every portfolio, knowing that a client brings their own unique needs and dreams along with every dollar. Furthermore, the company should lead you through the retirement income planning process so that every step is clear and well-defined. They should strive to go above and beyond in every aspect of their business.

Two of the signature traits you should look for in a company are independence and objectivity. There are two different kinds of people in the retirement planning business. The professional that most people are familiar with is the *registered representative*. These professionals are governed by FINRA and work on a commission basis, or a combination of commission and fees that are collected in "wrap" (fee-based) accounts. It is certainly conventional to work with these kinds of people, but it is not always the best choice. The sad truth is that these professionals work for themselves and for their companies—they do not work for you.

The basic problem with registered representatives is that they must work with a broker dealer. A broker dealer is a larger company such as a bank, brokerage house, wire house, or insurance company. These companies are governed by FINRA, so their only responsibility is to make sure that each sale is "suitable" before they can make the transaction; unlike independent advisors, they do not have a fiduciary responsibility to the client. In addition, broker dealers often limit their representatives to working with companies that they have relationships with. This handicaps the individual representatives and leaves them unable to work with the companies that they believe in. They may not be able to offer suitable options for their clients because they lack freedom; they are under the control of bureaucracy and sales quotas. Registered representatives simply have concerns other than the needs of the client.

Another problem with registered representatives is that they are commission-based, which creates incentives for the representatives that do not always mirror the needs of the clients.

I recommend someone different. Someone who doesn't answer to a broker dealer. They need to work for you, which means that your success is also theirs. Find a company that is completely independent and objective, and uses their knowledge to help their clients. There should be no strings attached and you should be in control.

You should strive for a company that shares fiduciary responsibility with you as the client. One who wants you to prosper, and whose incentive is your growing account.

Of course, the many details are confusing for common investors. Who should you trust? How much should you trust them? With so many different kinds of professionals in my field, it complicates the issue even further. Should you go to a new professional for every single worry? What is the difference between a stockbroker, a financial advisor, an insurance agent, an investment advisor, an investment representative, a registered representative, and a personal banker? It seems that these titles are used interchangeably by the uninformed public, but the truth is that certain services require certain titles.

For example, many of these designations—as we discussed earlier—have tremendous downsides. For instance, if you work with a broker dealer, there is a conflict of interest because broker dealers market their own products, leaving a wide potential for advice that is not autonomous from the broker-dealer's needs. There could be annuities or secondary offerings that are affecting the advice that that broker dealer is giving to you. Maybe that broker dealer has a selling arrangement with Mutual Fund "A" and not with "B". Does that mean that "A" is better than "B"? When working with a proper boutique firm you shouldn't be marketed those products. There should be no hidden agenda. With the focus on you, they can work towards finding the best way for you to retire and enjoy the fruits of your labor.

Again, their foundation should be independent and objective. The sad truth is that most people choose to go with one company or another because they don't understand the different registrations and organizations that exist in today's crowded marketplace. This is the part of investing that is often overlooked—the who behind the what. You will hear more about this in the following chapters.

Although past results are not a guarantee of future success, you should also make sure to choose a company that has developed a disciplined process that has worked over time. They need to do their best to ensure that clients can retire and remain retired; you should not find yourself desperate for a part-time emergency job when income fails at seventy-three. Find a company who specializes in maintaining security in the hardest economic time for retirees in history. Don't hire them to get rich, hire them to improve the likelihood that you won't go broke. With people living longer, circumstances have greatly changed. Interest rates are the lowest they have ever been, volatility is high, real estate is unsettled, and markets are unsure. Remember that in the last twelve years we have seen the stock market drop 50 percent twice, which is completely unheard of. Throughout all of this turmoil, companies exist that helped retired clients enjoy a beautiful quality of life.

Having the fundamentals in order, they should be able to run an organized business. Above all else, they should believe in educating their clients. This is an integral part of the process, and it should be based in pure honesty and resourcefulness. The added value of a company like this is that they take the time and consideration to make certain that every client is directly involved and has answers to every kind of question. During the creation of personalized strategies, they should help clients make decisions based on a broad spectrum of needs. Because they don't have shareholders to report to, their attention should be centered firmly on you, the client. The extent of a company's customer care should be reflected in life-long relationships; with an eye to your life now, they need to prepare you with sound options for the years to come. Though some clients like to give their professionals the task of making decisions, I urge you to find someone who makes it a priority to meet with you at least once per year and emphasizes a preference to meet on a quarterly basis. This allows them to monitor their clients' progress; focusing not only on your monetary well-being but on your overall satisfaction with their firm as well. Many professionals at other firms make a sale and never see their clients again. Clients often receive an annual company report and are expected to analyze it on their own. In my opinion, professionals should terminate their relationships if their clients don't make an effort to meet with them face-to-face once a year.

Strive to find someone whose practices are different. You should work with someone who makes a commitment to clients that is both professional and personal. In scheduled meetings, phone calls, and quarterly reviews, they should treat a variety of economic issues. No matter the size or complexity of the questions, you should be offered one-on-one consideration. A solid professional can help with car purchases, estate creation, Social Security changes, and budgeting woes. As a client you want to be able to rest easy knowing that you will receive prompt help from a professional you know. Some companies hold client-centered events such as business openings and anniversaries parties. These events are where they get to celebrate life landmarks and really get to know their clients. I believe things should be different. You should never get voice mails or busy signals, and you should always have your call returned the same day. Believe it or not these companies do exist and you should spend the time to find one for yourself.

Remember, there's a lot of misinformation on the Internet. No one should be expected to sift through all of it, let alone use such data to make important decisions. With so many scams and false advertisements out there, it is nearly impossible to navigate on your own. You want to work with a professional who knows how to help you. One who has successfully helped hundreds of people retire, and can feel proud of their satisfied clients.

Another important consideration when seeking a professional is they should not have custody of any of your assets. In other words, you should not need to worry about Bernie Madoff problems. People wrote personal checks to him and trusted Madoff with their money. Some people gave their entire life savings to Madoff Securities and lost it all. To protect you from this, your firm should not accept client-written checks. Instead, they should work with large, well-established, third-party companies that are well-situated to ride out economic storms. By doing so, the firm gives up the ability to pull money from your accounts. Instead, they use third-party custodians to hold people's money in great care. As a result, you as the client know that your money is safe with organizations that offer record keeping, statements, online access, and peace of mind.

One of the top benefits they should bring to the table is transparency. As stated earlier, many different kinds of investments contain hidden fees. This should never be the case. Many times the fees that you pay using independent firms come in at less than you are paying currently during your accumulation years. Additionally, the fee is often tax-deductible, which is not the case with many other investments. Be sure to check with your financial professional about the fees you are paying now before making any decisions.

Above all else, you should want to work with a company because they take care of all the details, and have unparalleled communication and customer service.

CHAPTER 6

Four Risks to Avoid at All Costs

1. **Longevity risk**
2. **Market risk**
3. **Retirement timing risk**
4. **Inflation risk**

WHEN YOU GO into retirement, you face a unique set of serious, real risks. If you don't address these risks, there may be consequences. The advice that most of you have been getting about retirement is toxic. Sadly, you could be lost if you don't choose to work with a specialist who can help you navigate the four risks listed above. Your financial professional should work with you to minimize these risks to the largest extent possible. Many of the big banks and advisory firms do not even bother to educate their clients about risk, which I feel is criminal. The company you choose to work with should make sure to educate you about the risks above, and I believe that the American public should be informed as well.

Before diving into each of the risks, I want to lay a framework by giving an overall summary of retirement income planning and why it is important. To start off, the most important thing about retirement income planning is that it is different from other types of income planning. The field is quite complicated and requires a great deal of planning and tailoring to the client's specific needs. The solutions your financial professional offers should be customized and dependent on your particular situation.

In order to help a client prepare for retirement, the professional in question needs to have a broad knowledge of what's going on in the world of retirement planning. This is not an easy job, and it is not for everyone. The job requires a great deal of customization because there is no one single approach that works for every client. Everyone's situation is different. Income and resources vary, circumstances vary, age of retirement varies, and even the client's views on retirement may vary. Some clients may want to work longer; others may want to make it a priority to play golf every day or get involved in a nonprofit. Every choice and particularity requires customization.

In order to help you construct and enjoy the new phase of your life, the company you choose has to hone in on a very specific skill set.

The biggest difference between the accumulation phase of investing and the retirement phase is that it's really difficult to recover from mistakes once you retire. You do not have as much time to recover once retired, and you also lack any sort of earned income. You no longer have the ability to just go out and make more money if needed. You do not have the luxury of money continually going into your 401(k) every week. Instead you must rely on income from your accounts, and once you have made a decision about where to put your money, it is hard to recover from any mistakes that might crop up.

Another important feature of retirement planning is that the plan needs constant review. Plans are very complicated and need to be modified as time passes. Your assets are a living, breathing creature, and you have to stay on top of what is transpiring with your money.

In summation, retirement planning is worlds apart from saving for retirement. For example, you could seriously undermine your plan by taking out too much money for an impulse buy. A mistake like that is very difficult to recover from. Other factors that may negatively impact your retirement, such as the sequence of returns, are going to pose a great threat. When you move from the growth phase to the retirement income phase, you are switching to a completely new task—another species of animal altogether. The question all baby boomers need to ask themselves is this: "Am I going to outlive my money or will my money outlive me?"

Longevity Risk

The first of the four risks that I am going to discuss in this chapter is longevity risk. What longevity risk means, simply put, is the risk of outliving your money. That is, of course, the common nightmare for folks heading into retirement. No one wants to end up broke and destitute at the end of his or her life.

Before we dive into the specifics of this risk, let's set up a basis for our discussion. That means discussing how long people are living these days.

I'll let you know up front that the situation is dire. Clients should be worried about longevity risk because no one can predict with certainty how long they will live. You and your spouse could both end up living decades longer than planned. Typically speaking, the wife will live longer, which means that whatever plan is in place has to apply to both spouses—it can't taper off once the husband dies.

If a client lives longer than the money in her retirement account, that can have a disastrous result; she will lose her income and may have to take on an emergency job or drastically downsize her lifestyle when she is quite advanced in age. This risk affects both couples and single people.

The first thing to know about longevity risk is that people are living longer than ever before because of advancements in health care and quality of life. The average lifespan has changed more in the last fifty years than in the last thousand years. This statistic may seem hard to believe, but it is true. There are many factors today that have contributed to this increase in life expectancy. For example, our health care system is better than ever before. Other amenities such as technology and climate control are only adding to this trend.

If you are sixty-five years old when you retire, the probability of living to eighty-five is 54 percent for males and 64 percent for females. That means twenty years of retirement in most cases. If you look at the probability of living to age ninety, the statistics are even more interesting. Thirty-three percent of sixty-five-year-old males and 34 percent of sixty-five-year-old females today will still be alive at ninety. In other words, one out of every three people who are retiring at sixty-five will still be alive at ninety. This means that you have to factor in for a twenty-five-year-plus retirement in order to be sure you don't outlive your money.

There are several misconceptions floating around about longevity risk, and they are very dangerous for potential retirees. There is a lot of misinformation regarding the safe harbor systematic withdrawal number. Most people who don't have access to the proper professionals, and who just try to plan their retirement by looking around online, will find that the average amount the experts are saying you can take out each year using the systematic withdrawal approach is now 4 percent. This means that if you have $1 million, you can withdraw $40,000 a year and you won't outlive your money. (Remember, the money in this case is adjusted for inflation.)

Unfortunately, this is flawed advice for a number of reasons. The *Journal of Financial Planning* recently put out a piece written by Manoj Athavale and Joseph M. Goebel, who both have PhDs and are professors of finance and insurance at the Miller College of Business at Ball State University.

Athavale and Goebel discuss what a safe withdrawal rate is using safe return distributions. Most people believe that the 4-percent rule is safe and will protect them from the risk of depleting their portfolio; however, as we discussed earlier, the 4-percent rule was based on Monte Carlo backdate testing and assumed fixed income rates that don't exist today. Practically speaking, there is absolutely no empirical evidence to support the theory that 4 percent is a safe rate of withdrawal. The companies and individuals championing this number lack any accurate data to support their conclusion.

Essentially, these two PhDs were able to show with unassailable accuracy that using a diversified stock portfolio and taking out 4 percent will fail about 20 percent of the time. The article shows clearly that the safe withdrawal rate is really 2.5 percent, not 4 percent. As if it needed to be said, there is a huge difference between 4 percent and 2.5 percent.

What this means, practically speaking, is that the same million-dollar client we were discussing earlier will have to live on 40 percent less income.

Now he or she will have to live on $25,200 a year instead of $40,000. This is going to be a challenge for retirees, because we are at the end of a sixty-year bull market. As interest rates go down, the prices of securities go up. Up until now, the environment has been good for retirees because interest rates were higher, but now they are at all-time lows. Even if interest rates were to go back up to 5 percent, there would still be challenges.

Longevity is the biggest risk of the four that we will be discussing in this chapter. You have to pay extremely careful attention to this risk, because you do not want to become a statistic.

In conclusion, to be safe you can only draw 2.5 percent per year. The 4-percent withdrawal rate is a myth. It is completely unsafe, but many planners still continue to give that advice. If you want a safe return rate and you don't want to run out of money, the number to look at is 2.5 percent. People have to understand that change. I know that it is a big dip and could be hard to manage, but the thing you do not want, above all else, is to see your portfolio fail.

One of the ways that your financial professional should work towards helping to reduce longevity risk is by looking into Social Security. One strategy I often find myself recommending is to have the client defer taking Social Security for as long as possible. One of the big fallacies going around in contemporary culture is that you have to take Social Security while you can get it, or the government will take it away. This is completely false. The fact of the matter is that Social Security won't be running a deficit for another twenty-five years. The way Social Security works is that, if the system is ever fundamentally changed, the changes will only affect future participants. People retiring from younger generations will have to wait longer and pay more into the fund.

However, any impending changes to Social Security absolutely will not affect those that are already retired. There's a big fallacy out there that you have to take the money right at sixty-two, but that is actually one of the biggest mistakes retirees can make.

Let's take the example of a couple that is earning a combined $60,000 of adjusted gross income before they retire. If that couple decided to take Social Security at age sixty-two, that would only replace 23 percent of their pre-retirement earnings. If they wait until sixty-six, which is four more years, then Social Security will replace 32 percent. What's more, if they wait until they are seventy, Social Security will replace almost half of their income, which is a significantly better deal.

Unless there is some significant reason that makes you think you will die early—such as a terminal illness—then you should seriously consider delaying Social Security. Think of it this way: each year that you wait to sign up, you are getting an 8 percent raise. That tactic is a good way to help you avoid longevity risk, because Social Security is something that will last until you pass away, no matter the age. Also, deferring Social Security helps with another one of the four major risks, inflation risk, because inflation is built in to the salary you are getting through Social Security.

A strategy I believe in, depending on the situation, is having retirees draw down their IRAs and 401(k)s in their early years to delay taking Social Security. By doing this, they can often afford to wait until the age of seventy to start taking Social Security. This strategy makes an awful lot of sense, because a 401(k) is not guaranteed to last your whole life, but Social Security is. If you use your 401(k) for income in the early years and delay Social Security, then by the time your Social Security kicks in at seventy, you only have to meet 50 percent of your income through other means. That means that your portfolio won't need to generate as much income, which means that you will have a better chance of not outliving your money. The firm you choose should be extremely capable of using strategies like this to address longevity risk.

Another strategy that is sometimes recommended, depending on the client, is to invest in a vehicle such as a fixed annuity that comes with a living benefit rider. We will go into that option more in the next chapter, but the investment will guarantee that the client will not outlive their money, which makes it a great way to reduce longevity risk.

An additional way to address longevity risk is through a flooring strategy. The firm you choose to work with should work with you to create an income floor that guarantees that all of your non-discretionary income will be there for you when you need it. They should work together with you to figure out what your basic needs are. These needs are the things that you cannot do without, and often include a mortgage, health care premiums, food, and car expenses. They should look at all the essentials that you need on a day-to-day basis, and establish a flooring strategy.

A flooring strategy is different from the systematic withdrawal approach, which doesn't guarantee that the income is going to be there for life. With the systematic withdrawal approach, you won't know whether the money will be there or not if you end up living beyond ninety, which, as we discussed earlier in this chapter, is becoming a much more common possibility.

With a flooring strategy, you know you're safe. For this strategy, an annuity can be used in combination with Social Security and any pension that you may have in order to create an income floor to cover essentials for both you and your spouse for as long as you both live. That will address the longevity risk and protect against fluctuations in the market. Then you can take the rest of the money and use a slightly riskier systematic approach. You can put that in the stock market. That way, if the market ends up being bad one year, it will not affect your life in a significant way. In a worst-case scenario you might end up not taking a cruise, or decide to take the grandkids to Six Flags instead of Disney World. That said, you don't want your ability to finance your essential needs to fluctuate without your control. The only way to be safe and to put to rest the fear of longevity risk is to use a flooring strategy that relies on annuities, living benefit riders, and Social Security. This strategy is solid, regardless of where the market goes.

Market Risk

The next risk to discuss is market risk. This is the risk that your securities will go down in value because the stock market takes a plunge. The interesting thing is that the fundamental piece of investment advice you always hear—that you must have diversification—does not always work to guard against market risk in retirement. This is yet another reason why the decumulation phase is so different from investing earlier in life.

The most fundamental thing to know about market risk is that diversifying does not always work. Take a look at how the market was in 2008. It did not matter if you were in international stocks, large company stocks, biotech, or even bonds. Every single asset class lost money that year—large companies, small companies, international investments, and even bonds. Diversification did not help anyone fight against market risk during 2008. The only vehicles that didn't lose money in 2008 were CDs, cash, and fixed annuities.

A financial recession is not by any means the only factor that could cause a dip in the stock market. In addition to the financial recession in 2008, there was the dot-com bubble bursting in 2000. A dip in the stock market could also be caused by a war, an outbreak of bird flu, or many other factors that are completely impossible to predict. In none of these circumstances will diversification help you. There are always events that drive stock prices to fall. The only defense against market risk is to utilize safe solutions such as CDs or annuities; the problem with CDs is they do not create income and, in short, it is important to avoid using an investment vehicle which doesn't protect against inflation.

As far as ways to protect against market risk, we tell people that when you are shifting from the accumulation to the retirement phase, there are tradeoffs that have to be made to create an optimal plan. When people are in the midst of their working life, what most of them are looking for are high investment returns; however, when you are talking about retirement income, that is not what you want to focus on. Most retirees should trade the slim possibility of high investment returns for safety. Yes, using that strategy, you may probably ultimately give up some returns, but market risk can be a big factor when you are retired, and the chance of high returns does not make that risk worth taking. It is better to trade off possibly getting that maximum potential return for safety in retirement. The chance of investment returns is not nearly as important as the predictability of income.

Many people who are retiring also think that what is really important is the access to funds and the ability to draw them all out if necessary. But the fact is that for safety and predictability, you need guarantees, which means that you have to give up some liquidity.

A definite mind shift is required when moving from the accumulation to decumulation phase. You have to train yourself not to worry about the market and what it is doing, and realize that the more safe and responsible thing to focus on is having a steady income. You need to protect yourself from market risk. I have no good news to offer people on that subject. No one can magically predict what the market is going to do. Market risk is a powerful risk that can hit you at any time, and you do not want to take that chance. However, if you are using the right financial professional, you will find there are many different solutions that work. No two clients are the same, but a qualified professional can structure a plan to substantially moderate market risk. For example a plan that uses fixed indexed annuities, along with a combination of other strategies, to protect against this risk may help.

Retirement Timing Risk

The third major risk that we will discuss in this chapter is retirement timing risk. I like to call this the "sequence of returns," and it is a risk that can gravely affect portfolio performance. When you choose to start taking income from your investment it can have a gigantic impact on how successful your retirement will be.

What if, for example, a client decides to retire right before a market correction or before an upswing in inflation? Changes in the market like this happen all of the time and there is nothing a client can do to predict that kind of change. How do you protect someone from that kind of risk? There is no way to know when a shift like that will happen. No one can tell you what is going to happen in the market on any given day, let alone throughout your retirement. No one has a crystal ball that can see into the future of the stock market. When coming up with solutions to create retirement income, your financial professional must also make sure that these solutions work to address the risks associated with the sequence of returns.

Take another look at the graph in Chapter 4. Even if you look at the exact same four returns, there will be certain retirees who do well and certain retirees who run out of money early. As you can see, the sequence of returns can have a giant and terrifyingly negative effect. You could have two clients who retire at different times with the same exact portfolios. By retiring one or two years apart, they ended up with completely different financial situations. How do you mitigate that risk?

This is where the flooring strategy comes in. The purpose of this strategy is to design a program to ensure that your non-discretionary income needs will be met. This can be accomplished through a plan that can be carefully devised for you by a proper professional using sources of income that are guaranteed by substantial insurance companies (not the federal government). I firmly believe that these sources of income will be there no matter what is going on in the stock market or the interest rate market. Guaranteed income can come from an annuity with a living benefit rider, Social Security, and pensions, which are guaranteed by the federal government. If you retire and the market suddenly loses 10, 20, or 30 percent that first year, what will you do? If you have a plan in place that does not allow you to lose your principal, then all of a sudden it does not matter what the market is doing during those first years; as long as you have a flooring system for non-discretionary needs, you will not be effected by a negative market.

Can the market affect your discretionary income? Yes. But you will also see the upside of the market in this part of your portfolio. If the market is not doing well, it is better to not take that Alaskan Cruise next fall than to have to sell your house or change the lifestyle that you have had for the last forty years. A proper specialist can help you minimize risk, but of course there is always going to be some amount of risk if you are leaving any portion of your income in the stock market.

Inflation Risk

The last risk is inflation risk. That is the risk that the amount of money you will need is going to grow because your purchasing power will decrease. You may remember that old cliché that a dollar is always worth more today than it will be tomorrow. That old saying holds true. Inflation risk should be a big concern. Some people think you can go to the stock market to combat this problem. That may have been true at certain times in the past, such as during the 1980–2000 bull market, but there have also been times in history when that wasn't true. For example, you would have lost purchasing power if you had invested in the market from the 1970s to the mid-1980s, so fighting inflation risk through the stock market did not work.

The inflation risk that clients face today is real, and they must seriously take it into consideration if they want to have a safe retirement. The good news is that a safeguard against inflation risk is built into Social Security, so some portion of every client's income will be built to take inflation into account. The bad news is that it is not possible to live on Social Security alone. You will need your retirement assets to supply income as well.

So the question becomes, what can a client do about inflation risk? One good option is a fixed annuity. A safeguard against inflation risk can be built into the system within the fixed annuity.

Certain fixed annuities will protect the client and offer increasing income during retirement years, guaranteed. Your financial professional can make sure to put inflation protection into the annuity products they use with their clients. That way, while you are not getting rid of the risk entirely, you are at the very least fighting it off; you have the guarantee that your income will go up.

The second thing you can do is to purchase Treasury Inflation Protection Securities (TIPS), which you can buy directly from the government. This is a guaranteed way to protect you from losing purchasing power. The interest rates of TIPS are directly linked to inflation, so they can make a great investment vehicle as part of a complete portfolio.

Another factor to think about when planning for inflation risk is that inflation always benefits people who own assets such as land and homes. I strongly advise my clients to own real estate or their own home. That way they have the option of using a reverse mortgage or tapping a home equity line as a way to fight inflation. They can also tap into their home equity to supplement their income tax-free, although these approaches have risks as well.

There are other major strategies that address most of these risks. One strategy is delaying retirement as long as possible. Many of you enjoy being in the work force, and those individuals should continue working part-time, especially during the early years of retirement. This can be a good way to ease into the new lifestyle of retirement, and it also puts less stress on your portfolio. You will be taking out fewer funds, and that makes a big difference.

The other strategy, which we discussed above, is to delay taking Social Security as long as possible, so that Social Security can work for you to replace more of your income. Another very good idea is to monitor your retirement plan, and, whenever possible, to decrease spending.

The third major strategy is the flooring strategy. That's one of the most important options that I have stressed here. If you use a flooring strategy, then you know that you have taken steps to insure that your income will provide for what you and your spouse need. This strategy will address market risk, retirement timing risk, and longevity risk. Furthermore, if you use a fixed annuity, you are also addressing inflation risk and the loss of purchasing power.

I want to stress again that it is not a good idea to use the systematic withdrawal approach for your essential income needs! That is just playing a guessing game with how much money you can take out. You do not know how long you will live, which makes that approach extremely dangerous. In addition, as the article in the *Journal of Financial Planning* shows, the safe rate is only 2.5 percent.

The last strategy is that you need to engage a professional planner, someone who specializes in retirement income planning. Find an expert, someone who can guide you to make the right decisions with your money, so that you are protected and provided for.

When it comes to retirement, you are at a time in life when there is little room for error. The combination of risks creates a puzzle that can only be solved by product diversification and working with someone who knows retirement income planning inside and out. That is a very important piece to remember. There is no one-size-fits-all company, product, or solution that will mitigate all these risks. You cannot merely depend on the stock market, which is the mistake that most people make. You have to use a combination of complex tools and strategies, ones that should be designed by a seasoned specialist. You must work with them to create a strong, flexible plan that will help you for the rest of your life.

CHAPTER 7

The Retirement Plan They Don't Want You to Know About

FIXED INDEX ANNUITIES are the only investment product that exists in the world that can give you increasing income on a depreciating asset.

Just think about that sentence, and how amazing that fact is. Fixed indexed annuities are a powerful tool for retirement planning. I believe they are part of a vital set of tools that many investors need to find a successful retirement solution. I cannot say the same for municipal bonds, banks (even people in FDIC banks lost money during the S&L crisis and the 2008 collapse), or government-sponsored enterprises such as Fannie Mae. Insurance companies, however, are required to have more liquidable assets on hand than the value of all polices in force.

As we have discussed in previous chapters, Wall Street's solution for secured retirement income is the variable annuity; however, variable annuities are often not a safe or helpful tool for retirement income investing. Say that you are fifty-five years old and ten years away from retirement. Even with a best-case scenario, using a variable annuity, you might be able to return 8 percent a year. The downside here is that when using variable annuities, all the investment and market risk is on the investor instead of the insurance company. Basically, what you are buying when you purchase a variable annuity is hope. You hope you will get that 8 percent, but you often fail to get anywhere near that figure.

Meanwhile, while you pray to achieve that fabled 8 percent, fees of at least 5 percent at the low end will handicap your investments.

Take a look at the following figure, which illustrates the difference between variable annuities and fixed indexed annuities:

Wall Street Solution:	Insurance Solution:
Variable Annuity	Fixed Indexed Annuity
55-year-old, 10-year deferral	55-year-old, 10-year deferral
$100,000 investment	$100,000 investment
8% IRR	0 Return! (worst case and not likely!)
5% fees (Management rider and MTE fees)	1.05%
5% withdraw rate on the GWB rider	7% withdraw rate Rider guaranteed on the GWB rider
=$6,700 annual income and NO raises (unless your account grows past what increasing income. you have taken out)	=$7,000 annual income + raises based on the indexed performance

As you can see in the above illustration, in about five years, a variable annuity will give you a 5-percent withdraw rate, which comes out in the end to $6,700. That sounds pretty good, but the problem is that this income does not adjust for inflation. As we talked about in previous chapters, inflation risk is one of the main risks clients face in retirement. Remember, in twenty years you will need $2.50 for every $1 you have today.

The number one concern baby boomers should have going into retirement should be loss of lifestyle, not loss of principal. The way you lose your lifestyle is through inflation risk and the loss of purchasing power. As of today, variable annuities do not have any way to grow your income based on CPI once you start taking money out of them. You have to get an even higher return than the year before or else you do not get a raise. The typical retiree couple will have a thirty-year retirement, and they need to have their money retain purchasing power throughout that time. To accomplish this, it is crucial that your money keeps up with the rate of inflation.

The fixed annuity, however, is a different story. This is a solution that assumes no growth, comes with little or no fees (if there is a fee on the rider, it is typically close to 1 percent), and can offer a guaranteed 7-percent withdrawal rate. On $100,000, that gives the client $7,000 in the *worst-case* scenario. A client who uses a fixed annuity can have increasing income and no chance of outliving their money. Even in the worst-case market scenario, a fixed annuity will come in first for the retiree.

You may still be asking yourself why you should use a fixed index annuity. I have witnessed with my own clients that using a fixed annuity as part of a retirement investment portfolio can address many of the income needs that baby boomers have.

First, I will start with the basics. As a retirement income planner, it is my business to manage uncertainty. The fact is that ten thousand people a day are retiring, which means that ten thousand people a day are making difficult decisions that could doom them financially for the rest of their lives. When I meet with baby boomers, I advise them that the advice they have been getting about retirement is toxic. Principal protection is not the issue.

One of the biggest risks that baby boomers will face is a loss of purchasing power. It may be hard for the general public to accept and believe that this will be one of the biggest risks they will face because they may have learned a different lesson as children. That is because their parents' generation had to worry more about principal protection, because they lived through the Great Depression in the 1920s. Some baby boomers find it hard to change over the focus of their worry because of what they have heard about retirement tactics from their parents.

But the fact is, baby boomers face a different set of challenges and risks that come from a different market and economic climate. The biggest risk for people retiring right now is failing to keep up with their lifestyle and losing purchasing power. Successful retirement is not about how much money you have, the rate of return, what the stock market is going to do, what the federal policy is, or even the current debt of the US government. These are concerns that have little to do with you or your retirement. What you are looking for in retirement is income for thirty years. Again, don't get distracted by all the other noise and nonsense that the media outlets have driven into your head. Retirement is all about income!

There are two outcomes you need to worry about with retirement. Either you will outlive your money or your money will outlive you. These are the only two possibilities. Your number one priority is to make sure that your money will outlive you. That is the essential goal you should be focused on as you begin planning for retirement.

You may ask how the fixed index annuity fits into this whole equation. A fixed index annuity is a contract between the investor and the insurance company. One of the great things about a fixed annuity is that the insurance company is taking on all of the risk instead of the baby boomer. Unlike a variable annuity, the retiree does not have to take on any risk, other than the risk that the insurance company might fail (which is why you should only work with well established, solid companies).

This means that the retiree does not have to face one of the worst risks of retirement: market risk.

With a fixed annuity, the baby boomer has full principal protection.

The contract period for a fixed annuity is usually between five and fifteen years, and the most common contract is ten years. You can either pay for the annuity with a lump sum, or in installments over time. Unlike a CD, where the investor's money is locked up the entire time, you can take out a percentage of your value without any surrender charges. This amount will vary based on contract and carrier, but our discussion here is about an average contract for a fixed annuity that you might receive. Typically speaking, the investor can take out 10 percent of their principal value each and every year. And many of these annuities are backed by the world's largest and most trustworthy insurance companies, and can only be sold by licensed professionals who receive product-specific training.

There is a big misconception about fixed annuities, which is that if the client dies while he or she holds the annuity, the insurance company gets to keep the money. This is a falsehood. There is no fixed annuity like that, or at least not one a competent professional would recommend. If the client should pass away, the money gets passed on to the contract owner's beneficiaries.

In a fixed annuity, you can choose to tie your returns to popular stocks, bonds, or commodity indexes. The index is used as a guide for your returns, but your money is not actually invested in the stock market. Typically speaking, many professionals use the S&P 500 or the NASDAQ-100; however, if the index is negative for that particular year, your account does not suffer a negative return.

What that means is that if the market loses 10 percent, you would get a zero for your rate of return for the year. If the market gets a positive 10 percent, you get a positive increase that year based on your terms.

One thing to remember is that with a fixed annuity, you will not get all the gains in the market; however, you do not need all the returns of an index when you do not suffer from market losses. If you are willing to give up some upside, then it is possible to protect your downside. The power of annual reset is also very important. What that means is that every year is a separate year in your contract. At the end of each contract year, your annuity's index values are automatically reset. That means this contract year's ending value becomes the next contract year's starting value. Annual reset also locks in any interest your contract earned during the year. It does not matter what happens over five or ten years, all that matters are those twelve months.

You will have some limits on how much you can make, which are called caps. There are also floors, which you cannot go below. Your floor is zero, because you cannot be negative. The cap is going to be different based on different products and contracts. Let's say for example that you had an annual cap of 10 percent. That means that you can't make more than a 10 percent return each year; however, if the market goes up to 6 percent, you will make all of the 6 percent. Another thing to remember is that the growth is tax-deferred, which means that you don't have to pay taxes on your interest while your money is still in the annuity.

I am going to use a hypothetical example of a client we will call John to illustrate this point. John decided to open an account and deposited $200,000[4] to open his account on March 23, 2008. John received a bonus just for signing up, which amounted to 10 percent of his account value. These bonuses are typical for this type of annuity, and the important thing to remember is that the bonus cannot be lost. That sum is protected, as is the principal.

John and his financial professional decided to tie his return to the S&P 500, which is the most popular index to choose. He had a cap of 2.8 percent per month. Now, during that first twelve-month time-frame, the S&P 500 lost 55.74 percent. However, because zero was John's hero, his beginning value and ending value were exactly the same. Therefore he still had his $220,000 in his account at the end of the year.

March 23, 2009, to March 22, 2010, is the next period that we will examine. John had a 20.3 percent return. He was able to make a total of $44,600

---

4 These hypothetical numbers are based on historical returns but not a guarantee of future results and have been rounded off to simplify the illustration.

that year, which was put into his account. Now his account was worth $264,600. So from March 23, 2008, to March 22, 2010, John was able to make a total of $64,600, which is a compounded rate of return for two years of 14.9 percent annually, without any risk to principal. Not bad during a recession!

Client Using a Fixed Annuity Tied to the S&P 500

Date	Market Activity	Client's Account Activity	Account Value
March 23, 2008	---	----	$220,000 (principal+10% bonus)
March 22, 2009	−55.74%	0%	$220,000
March 22, 2010	+41.67	+20.3%	$264,600

An important thing to remember is that there were no fees at all included in John's particular account.

Naysayers will say that fixed index annuities are bad products because you do not get 100 percent of the market growth. But let's take a look at another hypothetical example of someone decided to try his luck with the market during the exact same period. On March 22, 2008, he invested $200,000 in the S&P 500. During the first year, he lost 55.74 percent. That amounts to a $111,480 loss, which means he was left with $88,520 the next year. Because, for this investor, each year is not separate, and his principal is not protected, he had to start the year with the $88,520. From March 23, 2009, to March 22, 2010, the S&P 500 gained a positive 41.67 percent. So on the investor's current account value, he would have made $37,927 in profit that year. If you add that to his previous balance, that means he had $128,928.

Individual Investing Directly in the S&P 500[5]

Date	Market Activity	Client's Account Activity	Account Value
March 23, 2008	---	----	$200,000
March 22, 2009	-55.74%	-55.74%	$88,520
March 22, 2010	+41.67	+41.67	$128,928

[5]The exact numbers have been rounded off to simplify the illustration.

This investor started with $200,000, which is the same as John's hypothetical annuity. Both of them were investing during the exact same time frame. One ended up with $128,928, and their rate of return was -19.71 percent per year. The other client ended up with $264,000. That means there was a 50-percent difference between the ending values of the two portfolios. The reason for the difference is that within a fixed index annuity you can't have a negative return. When you replace negatives with zeros, you do not have to have high returns to get a decent overall return.

One of the reasons the fixed index annuities work is that they protect you from the downside of the market. It is interesting that even though you do not get absolutely all of the market growth, you can still have decent returns.

There are different insurance carriers who offer many different types of fixed annuities, but the most common index used is the S&P 500. Take a look at this graph, which is from one of the larger carriers who offer these types of contracts, American Equity:

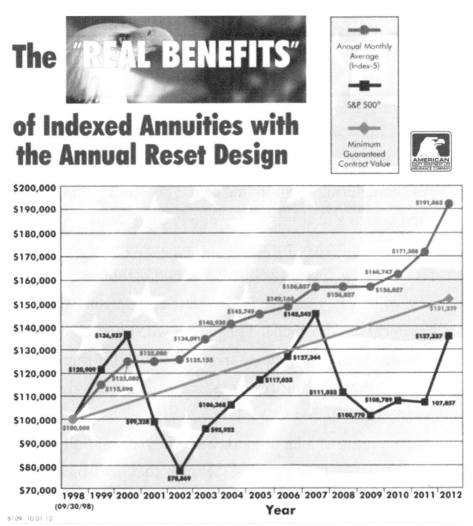

A history of American Equity's Index-5* (9/30/98 - 9/30/12)

*This graph is based on actual credited rates for the period shown on the Index-5 product, which is no longer available for sale. Past performance is not an indication of future results. Please call your American Equity Agent for new product information. Check out product disclosure for specific information.

"Standard & Poors®", "S&P®", "S&P500®"Standard&Poor's 500", and "500" are trademarks of the McGraw-Hill Companies, Inc. and have been licensed for use by American Equity Investment Life Insurance Company. This product is not sponsored, endorsed, sold or promoted by Standard & Poor's, and Standard & Poor's makes no representation regard the advisability of purchasing this product.

As you can see, the red line shows someone who invested in the market from 1998 to 2012. The line has dramatic ups and downs, and is a virtual roller coaster. The green line shows an investment in a fixed indexed annuity with the annual reset. You can see some pull back where the market lost a lot of value during the bursting of the dot-com bubble and the financial crisis. For about three years, the fixed annuity investor is not getting any returns, but is not losing anything either. As I said before, if you are willing to give up some of your upside, you can protect your downside. The person who invested in the fixed annuity's money stayed the same for three to five years during the recession in 2008. As the market rebounded in 2011 and 2012, they began to collect returns. The investor with the fixed annuity didn't need all the returns because they had protected their downside; their value stayed the same, and then the value went up.

Do you want to be on the red line with all the ups and downs of the market, or do you want to have no giant ups but no downs at all? Remember, you can never lose your principal or your bonus.

Another feature unique to these types of contracts is that once you earn interest, it cannot be lost due to stock market volatility. The fixed annuity can certainly be a less stressful option for the client. You do not have to watch the market, seeing your portfolio dip and dive, and hope that you will not lose anything. With a fixed index annuity, you know you are on solid ground.

Beyond everything that I have already talked about so far, the real power of the fixed annuity is that it does not have any fees by itself. You do not have to worry about trading costs, management fees, or any other type of hidden fees. Furthermore, a lot of the carriers offer living benefit riders that will help clients who are looking for guaranteed income when they retire.

The way that this rider works is that for an average fee of about 1 percent, the insurance company will give you contractual guarantees on top of everything else. The exact terms of these fees vary depending on the product and the contract. There's no point in going into the potential details of these riders in this book because we could talk about ten scenarios and by the time this book is printed, everything could be different.

What the riders do is that they guarantee that the person who invests the money will have a roll-up rate (or guaranteed increase for income) while waiting to retire, during the accumulation phase. Many companies, for example, will guarantee that during your deferral period, you will have a 7 percent guaranteed roll up every year if you don't touch your money. In other words, they will guarantee you a 7 percent increase every year for your income value. Let's look at what this would mean for a $100,000 account. Using this guarantee, we can accurately forecast that in ten years the account would have a minimum of $176,000 to withdraw as income. At this point, they will let you take out a specific percentage and guarantee that you won't outlive the money. If the stock market never had a return for the next ten years, then, without the benefit rider, you would be flat for ten years. At the end, with no benefit rider, you would only have $100,000 in your account because you can't lose what you started with. With the living benefit rider, the company will guarantee that your income value will go up to $176,000 and, not only that, guarantee that you can withdraw 5 percent of that value. And that withdrawal rate is guaranteed for life! On top of everything, the insurance company offers the option to receive increases in your income based on the CPI, which is a great way to measure inflation. Unlike the variable annuity where your returns will dictate raises, with the fixed index annuity, you can get raises based on the CPI. The other nice thing is that you can never outlive your money. Even if your account goes to zero, the insurance company is still on the hook to give you that monthly income for as long as you and your spouse are alive.

Another great benefit of the fixed annuity is that it is a great way to take an IRA, or Individual Retirement Account, and turn it into an account that is like a joint pension. Even if one spouse dies, the money is guaranteed for the other spouse. No mutual fund can do that for you, believe me.

If you started taking income out of that $176,000, your income would go up every year based on the CPI. Your account value could be going down because of your withdraws, but the income you are receiving is going up in line with the CPI.

A final benefit of the fixed index annuity is that when you pass away, whatever is left over goes to your beneficiaries. There is never going to be a situation where the insurance company keeps your money. Some contracts even guarantee a secondary tax-free benefit for your heirs, which provides an additional payout of up to 25 percent of all the gains you have acquired over the life of the contract. This way, even if you do spend down your account, there will always be something that goes to your heirs.

So those are some of the reasons why you and your financial professional should consider the use of fixed index annuities as an important component of your retirement investment portfolio.

CHAPTER 8

How to Cut the Government Out of Your IRA: Social Security Strategies You Probably Don't Know About

MOST PEOPLE THINK that you need to take Social Security as soon as you can; otherwise you will "miss out" on your entitlement to a system you paid into your entire life. This philosophy couldn't be farther from the truth. As a matter of fact, with people living longer and one of the major risks in retirement being inflation risk, Social Security is an important tool if leveraged properly.

In this chapter, I am going to discuss some outside-the-box strategies that can help you retire. Now, before I go into some of these Social Security strategies, it is important for you to understand that they only work if you delay taking Social Security until your full retirement age, which for most baby boomers is sixty-six. If you take Social Security early, at sixty-two for example, you cannot use these types of strategies.

Remember that one of the biggest risks that baby boomers have is outliving their money. The good news is that there are systems in place that help address this risk: one of these is Social Security. Now, most people out there will delay taking distributions from their IRAs and 401(k)s until they are forced to at age seventy and a half. These same people will claim Social Security as early as they can, typically at sixty-two. This is one of the biggest mistakes we see people making day in and day out. What guarantee do you have in your IRA and 401(k) that you will not outlive your money? How about protection against inflation? Social Security not only protects you from both of these risks, but also for every year you delay taking the benefits past your full retirement age, Social Security gives you an 8-percent raise plus cost of living adjustments! One strategy to utilize is to delay Social Security and spend down a portion of your IRA and 401(k) balances during those first few retirement years (from ages sixty-six to seventy). By doing this, you guarantee that Social Security will replace a larger portion of your income, and also reduce longevity risk. In addition, you have a built-in buffer for inflation through the CPI raises that are part of Social Security. Remember, you do not know if your IRA or 401(k) investments will last throughout your lifetime or if they will keep pace with inflation, but you do know that Social Security will do both. This is a simple solution to help your overall situation when looking at ways to maximize income and reduce retirement risks.

For many baby boomers, the wife does not have the same benefits as the husband because he worked longer and had higher wages paid into the system. Because of this, you can implement the "claim and suspend" strategy. This is actually a very simple way to maximize your income from Social Security and increase the net present value of benefits paid out. Let's say you have a husband and a wife and the husband is still working. The husband can apply for Social Security at full retirement age (sixty-six) and thus the wife would also be able to apply for her spousal benefit under him (typically half of his benefit). Now, because of changes in Social Security in 2000, he can actually "suspend" his Social Security while the wife continues to receive her spousal benefit. Because he has suspended his benefit, the husband's benefit base will grow 8 percent every year until full retirement age! Then at age seventy, the husband can reapply for Social Security and get a much larger payout. All the while, his wife has been able to collect even though her husband was not! Not only does this maximize what a husband and wife can receive from Social Security over their lifetimes, it also results in the highest possible widower benefit to the surviving spouse. Now, the husband may not want to work until age seventy, but even so with other assets to draw down such as the IRA, 401(k), and annuity, this plan can make a lot of sense and maximize his benefits, while minimizing longevity and inflation risks.

There are some baby boomer couples in which both spouses work and have Social Security benefits, so the "claim and suspend" strategy I explained above would not be ideal. A strategy you can use for this situation is called "claim now, claim more later."

Under the "claim now, claim more later" strategy, the client will choose the spousal benefit first, and defer the worker's benefit until later—typically age seventy. The higher-earning spouse will claim the spousal benefit under the lower-earning one. Simply put, let's assume that you have a husband whose benefits are $12k a year at age sixty-six and his wife's are $8k per year. The wife would apply for her benefits and the husband would then apply for the spousal benefits under hers; they would receive a total of $12k per year ($8k from hers and his 50 percent spousal benefit of $4k). Now, his Social Security benefit will continue to grow 8 percent a year up until age seventy. When he turns seventy he will then apply for his benefits, which will be $16k! Also keep in mind that when he passes away, his spouse will be eligible for the higher of the two benefits, so she will then collect his $16k. These strategies help increase the NPV for a client, Net Present Value of the annuity payments, which essentially is what Social Security is. Traditional thinking is to claim Social Security as early as one can and delay taking IRA and 401(k) distributions as long as possible, but I have just explained how this is actually the opposite of what you should do. Of course, if you have a short family lineage and don't expect to live past your early eighties, these strategies won't benefit you as much as someone who does because you would want to collect Social Security benefits as early as possible.

Most people have taken advantage of the 401(k) and IRA legislation by actively participating and contributing into these tax-deferred plans. What most people don't know, or simply don't realize, is that while these plans have been very effective in deferring taxes, they are horribly ineffective as inheritance vehicles. Did you realize there is a lien on your IRA? Yes, there is a lien of about 39.6 percent on your IRA, and the holder is the federal government. Let's assume you have an IRA. The balance on the account is $500,000, and your beneficiary is your only son. Did you realize that when you pass way, he will only get about $300,000 of that IRA? That doesn't take into consideration estate taxes (federal and state) or state income taxes! Why? Well, because whenever you take funds out of your IRA, which is a tax-deferred vehicle, they are taxed as ordinary income, not capital gains. This is troublesome and can cause your hard-saved dollars to be eaten up by the government. The good news is that there are strategies you can utilize now to protect yourself and family from this.

First, consider converting as much as you can into Roth IRAs during your retirement and working years. Roth IRAs do not require distributions and are passed on without income taxes because everything you take out is tax-free, as are the earnings. In other words, you can convert portions of your IRA each year and pay the income taxes now, as opposed to later. By doing so, when this asset passes on to your beneficiaries, it will be a net dollar for dollar inheritance without the burdensome problem of RMDs and heavy taxes. Each and every year, you should sit down with your advisor and tax professional to maximize the amount you can afford to convert without putting you into the next higher tax bracket. This strategy can have a major impact on inheritance. With the recent tax-law changes, regardless of your income level, everyone can convert to a Roth IRA or do partial conversions.

A second strategy that is not very common is to purchase permanent life insurance to replace the IRA or enhance the death benefit that your children or grandchildren will inherit. As a part of this strategy, you can even use your IRA distributions to pay for the new plan! One of the only assets that passes through an estate income tax-free is life insurance. The wealthy have been using it for years to successfully pay estate taxes and pass on more of their estate from generation to generation. Why shouldn't the average person do the same? Let's assume you are sixty years old and have an IRA with $500k in it. You could start to take distributions from the IRA and actually go out and purchase permanent, non-cancellable life insurance worth $1 million by simply taking the distributions and paying for the insurance each year. Think about that for leverage! The same IRA would have to grow to $1.7 million for us to replicate the net after tax result of the life insurance, and unlike most of the investments people make in their IRAs, this investment is guaranteed!

You may not like life insurance or life insurance companies, but I can tell you from first-hand experience that when you start doing the computations for the internal rate of return and account for taxes, fees, and management costs in the traditional investments you have been making, often life insurance blows them away. Now your stockbroker is very unlikely to tell you this, and as a matter of fact he will likely tell you to never invest in life insurance. He might say something like, "Life insurance is a way for the companies to make money and the agents to make a commission." He is either lying or greatly misinformed.

In 2012, I personally went in search of an investment vehicle for my own retirement portfolio and decided to use some outside-the-box thinking and apply it to the situation. I purchased a permanent second-to-die life insurance policy on my parents. This life insurance is permanent and as long as I pay the premiums, which can't be changed, I will stand to inherit a large sum of money, tax-free, when my last parent passes away. Of course I want them to live a long happy life, but unfortunately death is inevitable for all of us. The return analysis of this investment may shock you; take a look at the rate of return I would need to get in a traditional stock-like investment to equal the insurance payout at the age of the last parent's death:

Age Last Parent Passes Away	Annual Rate of Return
75	42.21%
80	20.92%
85	12.66%
90	8.42%

Remember, these returns are net of fees, expenses, and after taxes; in other words, you won't find a better place to put your money. If you owned an IRA and had to adjust these numbers for distributions, which are taxed as ordinary income, the returns above would be even higher! I personally own Roth IRAs and 401(k)s, but none of them can compete with the returns I have found on this life insurance investment. Life insurance provides a way to pass assets to others without subjecting them to the costs, delays, and uncertainties of probate. Life insurance is not susceptible to attacks on, or elections against, the insured's will, or the claims of creditors. Again, it's about thinking outside the box and working with a firm who can think outside the box for you.

CHAPTER 9

Working with Specialists Works

WORKING WITH SPECIALISTS is paramount to your success in retirement. Today's market is volatile, fast, and unforgiving. Working with a professional who adapts and stays current with the times will help you and your family navigate a whole host of retirement pitfalls. Choices that you make today will have an impact for the next twenty years on you and your family's life. The most important thing to remember is that your focus should be on income generation, not on accumulation or preservation of your asset.

When you are choosing a retirement professional, you should take a look at what makes that person or company different.

What should you look for in a retirement specialist? Let's say you had two different stocks you were thinking about investing in. One stock spent 100 percent of their marketing budget on marketing, and another stock spent 75 percent of their marketing budget on marketing and the other 25 percent on research, development, and education. Which stock would you buy? Most people would invest in the one that focuses some money on research and development. Working hard to make a stock more valuable and coming out with new ideas and innovations can make all the difference.

That is something you should look for with your professional. They should have a real commitment to research, development, and education. Look for someone who is dedicated to making their firm better and improving the education and skill of the advisors who work at the firm. Have they taken part in programs and classes at well known educational institutes? The company you choose to work with should be constantly bringing new ideas, concepts, and solutions to their client base. This may take years to trickle down to the retail client of a firm who is not constantly working to bring new ideas and changes to the forefront of their business. They should be spending a portion of their time every year on advanced continuing education conferences that cover topics such as investments, income planning, tax planning, and estate planning.

The analogy that I mentioned earlier in the book is important to remember. You go to your primary care physician, a generalist, when you have a basic issue or don't know what's wrong. If you are feeling sick, the PCP is a great person to see, but if you have a special need, you need to see a specialist. Retirement planning is definitely a unique situation where you do not under any circumstances want to be seeing a generalist. You need to sit down with someone who focuses on retirement income.

As I mentioned earlier, one credential to look for is the RICP® designation, which stands for Retirement Income Certified Professional®. "What is the RICP®?" you may ask. The RICP® is an advanced designation that makes sure that the advisor understands how to structure an effective retirement income plan that helps mitigate risks, and creates a substantial stream of income to last throughout a client's retirement years. It is very important to work with a specialist, and specifically someone who has that particular, high-quality designation. If you aren't working with a Retirement Income Certified Professional®, I believe you are working with the wrong person.

One way to find out if someone you are considering working with has the RICP® designation is to go to the website www.designationcheck.com. You can use this website as a resource to make sure you are working with someone who is an RICP®.

On a broad level, you want to make sure you work with someone who does not only have the minimum licenses mandated by various local and federal organizations such as the U.S. Securities and Exchange Commission (SEC) and the Financial Industry Regulatory Authority (FINRA). What you really want is to work with people who have gone one step further in that they have, at a minimum, a college degree. You want to make sure that the professional you work with has real, legitimate designations that require closed-course work and that are on the postgraduate level. You really want to be working with someone who has gone the extra step and has spent the extra money on research, education, and development.

To break it down, I believe the minimum designation you want to be working with is the RICP®. Beyond that designation, it is also important that the professional has a deep knowledge of the industry beyond the minimum requirements. If you really want to work with the best, you should work with a Certified Financial Planner® (CFP®) or Chartered Financial Consultant® (ChFC®). In the financial industry these are similar to having a board-certification. These designations both require over 500 hours of studies, minimum experience and knowledge, and closed-book proctored exams. The ChFC® designation has been a mark of excellence for financial planners for more than thirty years. This designation requires more courses than any other current designation. The curriculum covers extensive education and application training on all aspects of financial planning, income tax, estate, and retirement planning. You need to find someone who does not just meet the minimum requirements but who has gone out there and spent the time to gain as much knowledge as possible. You want someone who will go out there and do the best job possible for you and your hard-earned life savings.

Another analogy I like to use is that you've got the choice between two surgeons. One is board-certified, and the other is not. Which one do you want performing a life-threatening surgery on you? I would take the board-certified surgeon any day.

Last but not least, another designation to look out for when choosing a professional to work with you is the Certified Investment Management Analyst (CIMA®) certification. The CIMA® certification is "the only credential of its kind designed specifically for financial professionals who seek competency as an advanced investment consultant." There are actually three different exams required for the designation, and the first is a self-study entrance exam you have to pass in order to get in. As of 2013, the pass rate was only 57 percent for a first-time test taker into this program. Once accepted, this certification is taught at the Wharton School at University of Pennsylvania, which is one of the top three business schools. Topics covered in the school include modern portfolio theory, asset allocation, manager search and selection, investment policy, and performance measurement. CIMA® professionals "integrate a complex body of investment knowledge, ethically contributing to prudent investment decisions by providing objective advice and guidance to individual investors and institutional investors."

The other thing to note about the CIMA® designation is that their background check is the most rigorous that anyone could ever have to go through. The nice thing for potential clients is that if you are working with someone who has the CIMA® designation, you can be assured that their background was thoroughly investigated. The CIMA® designation is one of the hardest designations to achieve.

The bottom line is that it is not easy for investors to make their own quality retirement planning decisions today. Successful retirement planning is too complex, specialized, and challenging to be left to do-it-yourselfers and day traders.

The important thing to remember is that it is key to work with a specialist who at the bare minimum has the RICP® designation. If possible, look for someone who has the sought after certification of the CFP® or the ChFC®. On top of that, look for someone who has gone the extra mile and has received the CIMA® designation, which has the background check, requires you to apply to the Wharton School of Business, and is very difficult to get into. During the coursework for the CIMA® designation, professionals actually learn from the professors who write the books and appear on CNBC. You are learning from the brightest minds in the industry, and receiving the most cutting-edge ideas.

When it comes down to choosing a retirement planning professional, you want to work with someone who is specialized, knowledgeable, and educated, not someone who just has the licenses that are the bare minimum for the industry and who just wants to sell you a product. Find a professional who has put time into their own education and development and has the licenses and designations to go along with that. And remember to check www.designationcheck.com to make sure that the person you are dealing with actually has the designations they claim to have. This is a great site that explains to the public which designations are legitimate. If your professional does not have the designations and benefits that we have discussed here, it may be time to reevaluate whom you are working with.

CPSIA information can be obtained at www.ICGtesting.com
Printed in the USA
BVOW11*2358080115

382590BV00001B/1/P